Beneath the Veil of the Strange Verses

Studies in Violence, Mimesis, and Culture

SERIES EDITOR
William A. Johnsen

The Studies in Violence, Mimesis, and Culture Series examines issues related to the nexus of violence and religion in the genesis and maintenance of culture. It furthers the agenda of the Colloquium on Violence and Religion, an international association that draws inspiration from René Girard's mimetic hypothesis on the relationship between violence and religion, elaborated in a stunning series of books he has written over the last forty years. Readers interested in this area of research can also look to the association's journal, *Contagion: Journal of Violence, Mimesis, and Culture.*

Beneath the Veil of the Strange Verses

READING SCANDALOUS TEXTS

Jeremiah L. Alberg

Michigan State University Press · *East Lansing*

♾ The paper used in this publication meets the minimum requirements of ANSI/NISO Z39.48-1992 (R 1997) (Permanence of Paper).

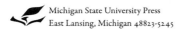 Michigan State University Press
East Lansing, Michigan 48823-5245

Printed and bound in the United States of America.

19 18 17 16 15 14 13   1 2 3 4 5 6 7 8 9 10

LIBRARY OF CONGRESS CATALOGING-IN-PUBLICATION DATA
Alberg, Jeremiah, 1957–
Beneath the veil of the strange verses : reading scandalous texts / Jeremiah L. Alberg.
p. cm. — (Studies in violence, mimesis, and culture series)
Includes bibliographical references and index.
ISBN 978-1-60917-364-7 (ebook) — ISBN 978-1-61186-076-4 (pbk. : alk. paper)
1. Philosophical anthropology. 2. Scandals. 3. Scandals in literature. 4. Violence. 5. Violence in the Bible. 6. Sacrifice. 7. Forgiveness. 8. Nietzsche, Friedrich Wilhelm, 1844–1900. Geburt der Tragvdie. 9. Dante Alighieri, 1265–1321. Inferno. 10. Rousseau, Jean-Jacques, 1712–1778. 11. O'Connor, Flannery—Criticism and interpretation. I. Title.
BD450.A45635 2013
808′.93353—dc23
2012028145

Book design by Charlie Sharp, Sharp Des!gns, Lansing, Michigan
Cover design by David Drummond, Salamander Design, www.salamanderhill.com.
Cover photograph, © Ernst Barlach Lizenzverwaltung Ratzeburg, is a detail of Magdeburger Ehrenmal by Ernst Barlach and is used with permission. All rights reserved.

g green press INITIATIVE Michigan State University Press is a member of the Green Press Initiative and is committed to developing and encouraging ecologically responsible publishing practices. For more information about the Green Press Initiative and the use of recycled paper in book publishing, please visit *www.greenpressinitiative.org*.

Visit Michigan State University Press at *www.msupress.org*

This book is dedicated in friendship to

Fr. Kevin Burke, S.J.

Br. William Rehg, S.J.

Fr. Aquinas Richard Schenk, O.P.

O you who have sound intellects,
look at the doctrine which hides itself
beneath the veil of the strange verses.

Inferno, IX, 61–63

Contents

In Christ God was reconciling the world to himself, not counting their trespasses against them and entrusting the message of reconciliation to us.

—1 Cor. 5:19

What is the word of reconciliation that we, Paul's addressees, are commissioned to speak in conversation with the secular scriptures of our modern era? It must be a word that opens the way back to the origin of those writings in God—in the primal and unfulfillable commandment to responsibility and in the primal act of forgiveness by which God has taken on himself all the pain of our failure to fulfill it. It must uncover the limit that makes the writing secular and by bringing to it the knowledge of what lies beyond, it must enable it to be recognized at last as a limit. It must, of course, impute no trespass. Rather it must accept the limit, it must read the point of trespass, the point which makes the writing secular, the point at which God is forgotten, as the point of forgiveness, the point at which God is incarnate, both revealed and hidden in flesh. Read as showing Christ in the moment which they mark themselves off from their origin in God, secular scriptures become the limit case of sacred scripture, the word of God no longer as an address to us—as God's reply to our prayer—but as the inarticulate groanings of the Spirit within us—as our prayer itself. These words (the word of reconciliation enables us to say) say what it is about us that needs to be redeemed. For, as St. Paul continues in his letter to the Romans, "we know that all things work together for good to them that love God" (8:28). Even in the works and words that seem to hide God's face, or to spit on it, we can see God revealed at the heart of our world and in our culture.

—Nicholas Boyle, Sacred and Secular Scriptures

Acknowledgments

The translation of Dante that I have used for my title comes from Prof. William Franke; it occurs in his work, *Dante's Interpretative Journey* (84). It is a book that I return to often and from which I always learn more. The long quote after the title page is used with kind permission from its author, Prof. Nicholas Boyle. Again, the whole work from which it was taken has been helpful to me.

There are three books from which I do not quote, and yet they have had a great influence on the way I conceived and wrote this book. So I would like to acknowledge Paul Griffiths' *Religious Reading: The Place of Reading in the Practice of Religion*, Alan Jacobs' *A Theology of Reading: The Hermeneutics of Love*, and Peter Ochs, *Peirce, Pragmatism and the Logic of Scripture*. Each in his way taught me something not only about reading but also about how one can share one's experience of it. Each transcends the boundaries of academic disciplines in a way that I find exemplary.

This book explores how an intelligent appropriation of mimetic theory leads to a hermeneutics of forgiveness, that is to an understanding of texts that might otherwise scandalize or wound consciousness in such a way that it actually contracts and becomes less able to take in certain realities. I show that the hermeneutics of mimetic theory allows our consciousness to take in more and more reality with less and less distortion. I first began learning about mimetic theory in the mid-1990s through the audiocassettes of Gil Bailie. There are thoughts expressed here as my own that I suspect actually originated with him but have become so engrained that I feel like I came up with them myself. I thank Gil and hope that I have not used them inappropriately.

As with all books there is a story behind the writing and publishing of this one. I will not relate that history here except to say that I had originally hoped to publish a collection of papers. The slightly dyspeptic reader who ended up with the unenviable task of wading through that stack of papers saw something more in them. With some acerbic comments he informed me of the work I would need to do in order to transform the disconnected pages into a book. I can only hope that the finished product approaches what he then imagined it could be. In the years since those first comments he has become my primary reader, critic, and friend. I am filled with gratitude to Prof. Andrew McKenna for all of his guidance.

Prof. Karin Sugano read an earlier incarnation of the work. I benefited greatly from her comments and criticisms. Karin's friendship over the years and many changes has been a great gift. Prof. Geneviève Souillac also read this version and helped me see ways of strengthening it.

Prof. Matthew Taylor read through the whole manuscript as it neared completion and gave much assistance by showing me how better to structure it.

Prof. Robert Snyder went through this book, scalpel in hand, eliminating my excess verbiage while pointing out my lapses in clarity. Each bit he removed, added something to the text; each lapse he helped me correct, reduced the obscurity. I am deeply in his debt.

I would like to thank my colleagues at International Christian University in Tokyo. In particular I have enjoyed and benefited greatly from my conversations with Prof. John Maher.

I have presented several of the chapters as papers at the annual meeting of the Colloquium on Violence & Religion and I am grateful for resulting discussions with the members of that organization.

The kind permission of publishers to use material is hereby acknowledged. A much earlier version of chapter 2 appeared as "Listening to Nietzsche" in *Revsita Portugesa de Filosofia* 57.4 (2001): 773–90. Topics found in chapter 3 have been much more extensively argued in my book *A Reinterpretation of*

Rousseau: A Religious System (New York: Palgrave, 2007). A section from chapter 5 has appeared in "Religiösen Leben in der Gegenwart" in *Zusammenleben der Religionen: Eine interreligious-interkulturelle Aufgabe der globalisierten Welt* (Berlin: Japanese-German Center, 2005). An earlier version of chapter 6 appears in *Violence, Desire, and the Sacred: Girard's Mimetic Theory Across the Disciplines* (New York: Continuum, 2012). All Scriptural quotations are taken from the *New Revised Standard Version*.

I am very proud to have this published in the Studies in Violence, Mimesis, and Culture series by Michigan State Press. I warmly thank the editor of this series, Prof. William A. Johnsen, for his patience as I revised the manuscript. I also appreciate all the efforts of the people at the Press to bring this book to light.

I continue to be grateful for the friendship of Prof. René Girard and his wife Martha. Finally, I wish that there were a way that this book could give to my wife, Yumi, a portion of what she has given to me during the writing of it. Instead I will try to remember to hang up the dish towel and put away my things. My daughters, Hannah and Yuriko, give me hope, and all three give me joy.

Introduction

Leontius and the Corpses

Mark Danner is a widely admired journalist for his reporting on world conflict. To introduce his recent book, *Stripping Bare the Body: Politics Violence War*,[1] he uses the following episode from Plato's *Republic*.

> Leontius, the son of Aglaeon, was going up from the Piraeus under the outside of the North Wall when he noticed corpses lying by the public executioner. He desired to look, but at the same time he was disgusted and made himself turn away; and for a while he struggled and covered his face. But finally, overpowered by the desire, he opened his eyes wide, ran toward the corpses and said: "Look, you damned wretches, take your fill of the fair sight."[2]

In an interview for *Harper's Magazine* Danner explains why he chose this passage. He sees the passage as dovetailing:

> with Leslie F. Manigat's observation that political violence "strips bare the social body," allowing us "to place the stethoscope and track the real life

beneath the skin." Manigat, who accepted power from the bloody hands of Duvalierist officers in the wake of 1987's spectacularly violent aborted election, argues, in effect, that this is no bad thing: that Leontius should shed his guilt and look long and hard. For to understand the real workings of a society, one must find a way to see beneath the surface, and the most effective way to do that is through the portal of political violence.[3]

"One must find a way to see beneath the surface." This suggests both the imperative and the challenge of a deeper gaze. Whereas Plato reports this episode as a kind of warning against giving in to the temptation to look, Danner suggests that in our culture one should be able to "shed his guilt and look long and hard." For Plato (and clearly for Leontius himself), Leontius's behavior is symptomatic of the failure of the rational part to control desire. Another force must be found that can align itself with reason so that reason can exercise its dominion over the passions. For Danner, in contrast, one must look, though merely gaping at the corpses is not enough.

Danner is correct, I believe, in seeing political violence as a privileged access or portal to what is going on in a society, but at least in this short introduction he merely identifies the problem rather than providing a way through it. That is, his recommendation for Leontius, and through him to us, to shed our guilt and look long and hard, does not tell us how one looks at the sight of murdered corpses in a way that is productive of deeper understanding. For Danner, looking represents progress over the guilt that would keep one from looking at all, but such progress depends upon the quality of the long and hard look. "One must find a way to see beneath the surface." Only then is the looking profitable and not harmful; only then do the corpses tell their tale of the "real workings of a society." Much of this book is about trying to see beneath the surface of a text, to "'track the real life'" beneath that surface.

How does one do that?

One begins to answer this question by developing an understanding of what precisely is going on when Leontius approaches the corpses. I use this scene from the *Republic* to describe what I will be calling a "scandal" or the "scandalous"—a surface or scene that both attracts and repels. The nature of the attraction and of the repulsion has to be made clear if a person is to avoid the danger that Danner suggests without naming: looking at the corpses and getting caught in the fascinating surface—against which it might indeed be better to shut our eyes, not to avoid seeing but to avoid being entrapped and thus losing the opportunity to "get beneath the surface." I say that Danner gestures toward this because he borrows from Manigat the image of a stethoscope, and one can imagine a doctor closing her eyes as she carefully "'track[s] the real life beneath the skin.'"[4]

The "scandalous" or "scandal," as I use it refers to those events, scenes, and representations to which we are attracted at the same moment that we are repelled. The scandalous is that which excites without satisfying, seduces without delivering, and promises without fulfilling. In one word it summarizes René Girard's analysis of mimetic desire as the doomed-to-be frustrated reaching for the *skandalon*, the object of scandal.[5] Mimetic desire is the desire that a person borrows or imitates from another. John wants something because Tom has indicated (usually by his own desire for or his possession of it) that he wants it. In and of itself this is not nefarious, but two factors combine to make it so. First, if two people desire the same object, then the stage is set for conflict. Not every object can be shared. Second, and this flows from the first, each of the antagonists will convince himself that his own desire was spontaneous, not imitative, and so, if not temporally prior, then at least having equal right to the object. In his first work, *Deceit, Desire and the Novel*, Girard called this belief the "romantic lie."[6]

Believing the lie about our own desire is neither innocent nor trivial. It is the starting point of the process of rivalry that eventually leads to scapegoating and violence. Neither party can see that the one desires the object precisely because the other does and vice versa. Both reach for it and frustrate the other's desire in so reaching. The first lie is each person's belief in the priority of his or her respective desire over the other's. At this primitive level of wanting and reaching for the same thing, how does one decide who gets what or who *should* get it? Each has an equal claim. Some form of violent resolution becomes inevitable.

This small conflict grows as more and more members of the community are drawn into the mimetic phenomenon of violence. Here is the second and more damaging of the lies: the other is responsible for this violence that the community is now suffering; therefore, the first person sees himself as innocent. Innocent because he believes that the desire was his alone and has priority over the other's. Therefore, his violence against the other is good, and the other's is evil. The other and his violence must be violently expelled.

This expulsion confirms the first's priority over the other. It thereby confirms the goodness of his violence and constitutes this violence as a transcendent force in that it brings order to the community.

In this process, scandal is the way that object becomes desirable at the very moment it becomes inaccessible, because it becomes desirable through the desire of another who either already possesses it or is a rival for its possession. This kind of scandal is a double-edged sword; it can entrap us, but it also can also be an occasion for a deeper entry into the truth. Scandal is the place where the battle between staying with the illusion or looking long and hard at reality is played out. I seek out this place in a number of different texts (both secular and sacred) to see how the author and the reader engage in this struggle.

In my first chapter I show that it is not something inherent in the scene of corpses or similar phenomena that is capable of scandalizing us. It is not something "out there" that gives an event this kind of power. But neither is scandal merely subjective. It occupies a middle ground that suggests that we, the spectators, bring something to the scene that gives it the peculiar quality we denote by the word "scandal."

I then propose that rivalry with another is the necessary element in any scandal. The rivalry does not have to be with those who are the object of our gaze (Leontius is not in rivalry with the corpses). I will analyze our everyday understanding of scandals—Watergate, clergy child abuse, celebrities behaving badly—to show that a kind of rivalry exists over the granting of access or the blocking of access to some promised reality.

This interplay of proffered access being contested by the blocking of that same access is traced back to the way language and thus consciousness itself operates. Ultimately, again with the help of the thought of Girard, it is traced back to the victims of violence, the very victims that Leontius struggled against looking at, and at whom Danner urges us to look, long and hard.

Friedrich Nietzsche, not unlike Danner, would have us look long and hard at the victim, especially the hero as victim in ancient Greek tragedy. Unlike Danner, however, Nietzsche does not point our gaze in this direction in order to help us get beneath the surface. On the contrary, he does it explicitly to make sure that one's eyes remain fascinated and enthralled by images of the hero's destruction. Nietzsche brilliantly describes the duality of longing and desire. He shows how desires are both rooted in sacrificial violence and give birth to scenes that manage to entrance the eyes so that we remain on the surface, never fully aware of what is happening. In *The Birth of Tragedy Out of the Spirit of Music* Nietzsche expels the only real revelatory power of Greek tragedy—namely, that its origin lies in the sacrificial victim from whom flows not just political order but culture as well. Nietzsche wants us to gaze enthralled and begin the sacrifice anew.

We turn from Nietzsche to Jean-Jacques Rousseau, because in a paradoxical way Rousseau holds the key of knowledge for looking beneath the surface—the paradox is that he holds it not unlike the lawyers in Luke's Gospel (ch. 11), declining to enter himself and preventing others from entering. As with every thing scandalous, it is a question of access and its being blocked. Rousseau sees, and would have us look long and hard at, the "scoundrel on the rack." He does this to convince us that, for the sake of political order—that is, to control violence—the scoundrel must remain on the rack. However, in the same argument Rousseau identifies the scoundrel with Christ on the Cross, thus transforming the scoundrel into a "scandalous sight." Rousseau does not want either himself or his reader to reach the place that Jesus pronounced blessed: the place where one finds no scandal in Christ. Rather, he would like to bind his reader in a scandalous relationship with himself, both offering and denying access to that privileged place.

This pairing of Nietzsche and Rousseau has been done before, most strikingly by Jacques Derrida,[7] who sees these precursors as representing "two interpretations of interpretation."[8] In my understanding Derrida is opposing Rousseau to Nietzsche to show that human beings interpret either by looking "for the lost or impossible presence of the absent origin" or by turning away from this search and affirming the play of interpretation. Rousseau is the sad representative of the former tendency and Nietzsche the gay representative of the latter. Derrida himself does not and cannot choose between the two. Ultimately I suspect that he cannot choose because there is no real difference. In my opinion Rousseau offers a clearer view of what is at stake, and so I use him as a way of suggesting that the ultimate reality that is being both opened up and closed off by these two thinkers is the reality of forgiveness in Jesus Christ. I think it comes out clearly in Rousseau that his aim is for the reader to remain frozen looking at the scandalous sight of the scoundrel on the rack.

Dante knew the danger of being frozen in such a position, but he used a different metaphor—that of being petrified. He was deeply aware of the danger of being turned to stone on an intellectual or moral level or, more precisely, on that level where the moral and intellectual overlap. It might appear that Dante is the polar opposite of Danner in that he recommends not only closing one's eyes but even allowing them to be covered to avoid gazing at certain scandalous spectacles. The intended goal, however, is the same—to get beneath the surface and "track the real life beneath the skin."

The closing of one's eyes to the surface can allow one to see the depths. If our journey here is an interpretive one, then different strategies are going to be called for in different situations. When we are stuck in this journey with no way forward and are threatened with the petrifaction of our hearts and minds, Dante's advice is to close our eyes and look beneath the surface. He is telling us not to get stuck on the scandalous, literal surface but to delve beneath it to the figurative meaning.

How do we get beneath the surface? The Gospels themselves contain an extraordinary pedagogy for reading. The real heart of this book is its fifth chapter on learning how to read. Jesus himself asks this question of the lawyer in leading up to the parable of the Good Samaritan: "How do you read?" We can expect that the answer to this question is somehow also contained in the parable. This is what I try to show.

The final chapter may come as a surprise. It analyzes, in effect, how Flannery O'Connor handled Leontius's situation. For O'Connor, fiction was all about teaching the reader to see reality as it is. She was, however, also aware of scandal, of the obstacles to seeing that come from the culture in which we find ourselves as well as those contained in the Christian message. Her artistic response is complex and, I would argue, left unfinished by her early death. But that is precisely why it is appropriate to end with her response, which helps us to grasp that our own struggle with scandal is an ongoing and unfinished one.

CHAPTER 1

The Language of Scandal
and the Scandal of Language

Leontius and the Corpses

Let's begin by looking more carefully at the surface of the episode from the *Republic* in which Leontius desires to both look and not look at the executed corpses he is passing by. This encounter is decidedly not a psychological conflict of desires. His desire to look at the corpses and not to look is not like my desire both to eat chocolate cake and not eat it, since I am on a diet. In the latter case either act has its pros and its cons. The chocolate cake will taste good; it may even taste all the better, being the "guilty pleasure" that it is. It will satisfy my hunger, but it will also leave me feeling like a failure and will contribute to my weight gain. Not eating will leave me hungry but also happy that I was able to control my appetite. I will not gain weight and might even lose a pound. When Leontius desires both to look and not to look, he cannot say what looking will do for him nor what not looking will deprive him of. The chocolate cake does not both attract and repulse me; instead, the cake and the diet appeal to two distinct goals: satisfying hunger versus controlling my appetite. The corpses attract and repulse in equal measure because they appeal to one goal: the "real workings of society" in Danner's formulation, the "truth of the victim" in mine.

So Leontius's encounter with the corpses is not exactly akin to "rubber-necking" as one drives by the scene of a traffic accident. Something else is going on here. Without pressing too hard on this short incident, we can pay attention to details we might have missed. First, the corpses are there not as the result of some accident but rather due to a state execution. Plato is saying that if one goes up from the Piraeus, with all of its significations as the site of this famous dialogue, one will come across things—executed corpses—that will trip one up. One will recognize what these kind of things are because they will have the peculiar effect of both attracting and repulsing. According to Plato, this kind of encounter is both harmful to the soul and the price one pays for practicing politics.

Second, Leontius's interior struggle is resolved by his giving in to the disgusting desire in the hope that the disgust itself will finally outweigh the desire, and so the latter will somehow not show itself again. What is it that Leontius wants to see? How is it that the corpses seem to beckon Leontius's gaze? A look at the victims of violence seems to promise access to some deeper mystery, yet Leontius also knows that simply gazing at the corpses will tell him nothing. Still, he cannot look away.

Plato, through the figure of Socrates, suggests that we should not look directly at the victim, even as he acknowledges that the victim at least seems to promise us a deeper, darker knowledge. To be a good citizen is to use the spirited part of the soul, anger in fact, to curb these kinds of desires and let the rational part rule, which means not only that this form of rationality cannot take in the victim but that it depends upon anger to function properly.[1]

All of this is true but it could be that Plato has more to tell us. The story that Socrates says he trusts is often read as a story of a struggle interior to the soul of the individual Leontius. He seems to be struggling with himself about a desire to look at a disgusting sight. Is this a sufficient understanding?

Leontius says, in fact, and this is the third point, that he "saw the executioner with some corpses beside him." That is, Leontius saw more than the corpses. In a story like this, we do well to assume that every detail is there for a reason. We do even better to assume that any detail we and others habitually pass over probably has some significance. No one comments on the presence of the executioner. In the text he is called "he who belongs to the people."[2] Now there are many interpretations that we could attempt here, all of them highly speculative. Plato suggests by his inclusion of the figure of the executioner in this story that the interpersonal dimension is critical—especially in situations like Leontius's that appear to be purely internal struggles.

Leontius longs to look and is disgusted with himself for longing. We sense that the more disgusted he is with himself, the stronger his urge to look; and, of course, the stronger his urge, the greater his disgust. Somehow the longing and the disgust mutually reinforce each other. This kind of encounter is a good example of what I mean when I use the word "scandal" and its cognates in this book. A scandal is an event that simultaneously attracts and repels us. A scandal is able to attract us precisely to the degree that it repels us and vice versa.

An essential element in scandal, beyond the struggle internal to an individual, is the interpersonal dimension between the man who belongs to the people and Leontius, the man who seems to want to belong to himself and fails. At this point we might even say that this is a hidden rivalry that constitutes the scandal.

A deeper understanding of the conflicted desire to see the corpses at the foot of the executioner will help us understand what it is we see when we look there. It will help us, then, to see beneath the surface of the corpses. The desire to look and not to look can be described as scandalous, and it is this conflicted desire that constitutes the sight itself as scandalous. But the desire is not conflicted "in itself," as it were. The conflict is always between persons. The desire is conflicted because a model is somehow communicating to the subject both "Look!" and "Turn away!" Although the word "scandal" is not Plato's, coming as it does from a strictly biblical provenance,[3] it still seems to capture well what the episode illustrates.

Plato is aware of the deep pull that the scandalous vision of the victim exerts on our consciousness. I think he is even vaguely aware that this pull indicates the central role that this particular scandalous vision of the corpse plays in the formation of human consciousness, in our uncanny desire both to see and not see when it comes to violence in our world. He also gives us a warning that we would ignore at our peril: the desire to look at that scene can produce, if not insanity, at least a spasm of madness. How else can one construe the words that Leontius addresses to his own eyes, "Look, you damned wretches, take your fill of the fair sight." This suggests a need either to master the desire, as Leontius could not, or to form our vision in such a way that it can bear the sight of the victim without scandal. I am suggesting that the only way that the latter can occur is by comprehending more deeply the rivalrous relationship that gives birth to the conflicted desire.

The thesis that guides this investigation includes a general definition of scandal in terms of a mediator who promises access to something and, at the same time, blocks it. Then we look at how scandal inheres in language itself and how it generates a kind of meaning. Language is the most human phenomenon; by which I mean most humans spend a great deal of time holding conversations, listening to lectures, watching movies with dialogue, or reading books, and animals do not. Thus, it is an anthropological phenomenon. From this fundamental, anthropological level we will be able to move to other ways that scandal affects us in interpreting texts, art, and, indeed, life itself.

Scandal, Rivalry, and Idolatry

We all know, even if we might not be able to formulate it in an exact definition, what the word "scandal" means. We see it used daily on the news and in the papers. In all that follows, I do not want to lose sight of this pre-understanding. It forms the background to our way of thinking about these things, and, if that way is to change, the pre-understanding needs to be made more conscious. Precisely because my thesis may seem quite divorced from our everyday understanding of scandal, I want to show that it is, in fact, deeply related to it.[4]

Scandal is difficult to define because it is never univocal. It always refers both to the scandal*izing* event—the Watergate scandal—and to the scandal-*ized* reaction of the public—the nation's shock at Nixon's abuse of power. Clearly the two references are related, yet they remain distinguishable. Beyond both the event and the reaction is the rivalry, usually hidden, that transforms a crime into a scandal. Scandals proliferate in our society because rivalry has proliferated. A rivalrous consciousness is prone to scandal, and scandal forms the consciousness.

Scandal occurs when someone simultaneously blocks access to something that he has also designated as desirable. In order for this to occur, in other words, in order that one person can in his or her relation with another person both offer and block access to something, there has to be a rivalry between the two. By rivalry I mean not just simple competition but a relationship that consists in the kind of admiration that makes the one want to have what the other has, that makes the one want to be like the other, and, simultaneously, in the kind of envy that makes the one hate the other for having what she has and for being who she is. When envy and rivalry move to the level at which a person can be envious of the other for who he or she *is*, then we have a situation that can be called idolatry. Idolatry is defined as giving power over oneself to another who otherwise would not possess that power. To want to be another person is to want the being of the other and to think that somehow that person could bestow it. Thus, the one to whom the power has been accorded to both grant and deny access to this being is the one who is able to scandalize; he or she is the *skandalon*, the idol.

My thesis is that revealing the rivalry and idolatry that underlie the scandal uncovers a way of forgiving the rivalry and idolatry so that the scandal becomes a bridge to deeper understanding. I want to apply this to the way that we read. Everyone can point to scandalous texts that offend, upset, or shock; and everyone can point to so-called prudes who are offended, upset, or shocked by texts that may or may not be in and of themselves scandalous. It is rare, however, for an interpreter to recognize the rivalry represented in the text that underlies the scandal.

Scandal is defined here in a way that makes clear its essentially interpersonal character. Although we often speak of scandal as if it were a thing out there, and although we talk about scandals as if they did not involve our own reactions to them, this is misleading because scandals depend upon rivalry for their existence. On the other hand, if we played a word-association game with "scandal," I doubt that the words "access" and "block" would come up, and so in this sense my definition does not correspond immediately to our everyday use.

Nevertheless, I think that this definition does include our everyday use of the word in that the scandals regularly reported in the news—e.g., clerical sexual abuse of minors, bishops covering up the abuse, politicians accepting bribes—involve a kind of promise of access and then a blocking of what has been promised.

The "promised" aspect of the phenomenon points to the relation between the office holder, for example, and the public. The public invests the former with the power to bring certain symbolic realities into existence. The failure to do so need not be scandalous; it could be merely disappointing.

It becomes offensive only when there is also an element of rivalry between the holder of the office and the public so that the public can see itself as the "victim" of an abuse of power or of the privilege that comes with the office. In other words, only when the public can see themselves, or someone very like themselves, as holding the office does scandal become possible. This helps us to understand the otherwise perplexing phenomenon of proliferating scandal in an era and culture of lessening taboos. It is more and more difficult to genuinely shock the public by some outrageous act, and there are fewer and fewer social taboos to violate. Scandals nevertheless increase more and more because everyone becomes the rival to everyone else.

When a man or woman in public office does something that contravenes what the office symbolizes, the promised access to a value-laden reality is, in fact, blocked or obstructed by the behavior. That which is supposed to be brought near is actually pushed further away, but what drives the scandal is the secret thought, "I could do it better." It would seem as though the stronger the symbolic nature of the office—for example, the President of the United States versus the mayor of Detroit, or a cardinal of the Catholic Church versus a parish priest—and the more egregious the offense, the greater the scandal would be, but this is to ignore the crucial interpersonal dimension in favor of a more "objective" view. If the world were so structured that a person could never imagine being royalty, then the misbehavior of the royals would not scandalize that person. But when the distance between commoners and royalty is decreased but not abolished, any infraction of the social order is seen as scandalous. We are most scandalized by those whom we most rival, by those whom we would most like to be. Moreover, in a perverse twist, scandal itself activates and generates rivalry, whereas before there was merely disinterest or indifference.

The "promise of access" is another way of saying that scandal has a seductive side. The public does not invest by accident this power in an office or the person occupying it. Good politicians use this kind of promise to attract followers. The blocking of the access that has been promised means that scandal is also always a bit of a shock. Further, it is precisely the distancing of what seemed to be offered that fans the desire. The dialectic of proffered and refused access gives scandal its particular quality of brandishing something attractive and always keeping it just out of reach. It accounts then for scandal's continual ability to fascinate.

Language as Scandalous

Although there is no lack of scandal in our world, it may still strike some as a secondary phenomenon, relegated for the most part to the edges of respectability. There is some truth in this. Our news media are not filled with scandals from one end to another. It is a not a scandal when a thief robs a bank, only when the president of the bank does, and I would surmise that more banks are robbed by ordinary thieves than by their own officers. Also, most of us have a low regard for those tabloids that treat scandal as their main attraction. Ignoring a scandal that may be titillating but insignificant or treating an otherwise scandalous incident with a degree of decorum helps to make certain media outlets "respectable." Although it has certainly been blurred, we still retain the distinction between "yellow" and "mainstream" journalism.

As the example from Plato shows, however, some of our greatest cultural achievements, like the *Republic*, have had to examine the phenomenon of scandal. Further, as Danner suggests, if today we are to "find a way to see beneath the surface," we need to have a clear understanding of what is fixating our view on the surface. To understand the centrality of scandal, as a social phenomenon and thus as a condition of our knowing, we need to look at language.

Reality becomes known and apprehended by humans only when it is named. Children clearly see things but still are driven to ask "What is this?" They do not seek an explanation but a name. Naming reveals the mystery of reality that manifests itself. I use the word "mystery" in the way we use it when we say that love is a mystery—not that it is unknown but that it is unfathomable, that with love there is always more to be known, grasped, and appreciated. Love, like reality and language, cannot be reduced to a formula. To name something is not to explain it away but to grant access to its mystery.

Normally we approach phenomena as something-to-be-explained. By "explained" we mean some sort of causal account. We list a series of space-time events to show how state A led to state B that then led to state C, the phenomenon we were seeking to grasp. This approach works well in most circumstances and is far preferable to seeking out occult answers or magical influences.

When this approach is applied to language, however, it is implicitly assumed that language is basically the same type of phenomenon as all other space-time events that we encounter. So we normally construe language to be made up of sounds that someone speaks and that bounce off the eardrums of the listener, stimulating nerves such that the same thought as was in the thinker's head is now in the listener's. But this is not language. Instead, it is communication, the kind that takes place among a large variety of animals.

Language is something altogether different. The signals by which animals communicate direct another animal's attention to something else—to food, to a predator, etc.—but words do not simply direct attention. Words mean something. A word "somehow comes to contain within itself the thing it means."[5] This, surprisingly, is a scandalous aspect of language. American novelist Walker Percy explains:

> If the relation of symbol to thing symbolized be considered as anything other than a sign calling forth a response, then this relation is "wrong." Say whatever you like about a pencil, Korzybski used to say, but never say it is a pencil. The word is not the thing, said Chase; you can't eat the word *oyster*. According to some semanticists, the advent of symbolization is a major calamity in the history of the human race. Their predicament is not without its comic aspects. Here are scientists occupied with a subject matter of which they, the scientists, disapprove. For the sad fact is that we shall continue to say "This is a pencil" rather than "This object I shall refer to in the future by the sound *pencil*."[6]

The word or the sound uttered does not function in the same way as a sign calling forth a response. Say the word "ball" to a dog and he will *react* by looking for the ball. If I say the word to a friend, she will look at me oddly and ask, "What ball?" Ignoring this difference of function is to ignore an essential feature of human language. Drawing again on Percy, "The word *names* something. The symbol symbolizes something. Symbolization is qualitatively different from sign behavior; the thing that distinguishes man is his ability to symbolize his experience rather than simply respond to it."[7]

This act of naming is scandalous insofar as one approaches it with the attitude that it is just like all the other phenomena that we encounter in the world. The scandal felt by semanticists and semioticists is not entirely misplaced. The phenomenon of language truly is extraordinary. The word "ball" is not a round object but nonetheless is. If words do not become in some way the thing to which they refer, then we cannot know the thing itself. Children *see* the object, they want for nothing on the empirical level, and yet they are insistent: "What is it?" They need a name to know the object. Hence the paradox that words are and are not their referents.

To enter more deeply into the nature of language's scandal, I quote from Helen Keller's autobiography. The familiar anecdote concerns her breakthrough to language:

> We walked down the path to the well-house, attracted by the fragrance of the honeysuckle with which it was covered. Someone was drawing water and my teacher placed my hand under the spout. As the cool stream gushed over one hand she spelled into the other the word *water*, first slowly and then rapidly. I stood still, my whole attention fixed upon the motions of her fingers. Suddenly I felt a misty consciousness as of something forgotten—a thrill of returning thought; and somehow the mystery of language was revealed to me. I knew then, that "w-a-t-e-r" meant the wonderful cool something that was flowing over my hand. The living word awakened my soul, giving it light, hope, joy, set it free! There were barriers still, it is true, but barriers that could in time be swept away.
>
> I left the well-house eager to learn. Everything had a name, and each name gave birth to a new thought. As we returned to the house every object which I touched seemed to quiver with life. That was because I saw everything with the strange new sight that had come to me. On entering the door I remembered the doll I had broken. [Helen had earlier destroyed a doll in a fit of temper.] I felt my way to the hearth and picked up the pieces. I tried vainly to put them together. Then my eyes filled with tears; for I realized what I had done, and for the first time I felt repentance and sorrow.
>
> I learned a great many new words that day. I do not remember what they all were; but I do know that *mother, father, sister, teacher* were among them—words that were to make the world blossom for me, "like Aaron's rod with flowers." It would have been difficult to find a happier child than I was as I lay in my crib at the close of that eventful day and lived over the joys it had brought me, and for the first time longed for a new day to come.[8]

I would like to dwell on this passage for a moment, for we are at the heart of the mystery. This is Helen Keller's breakthrough to language, which each human child makes between the ages of two and three but which no animal has ever made. Yet, if we listen to her, it was not a breakthrough to something completely new. Instead, it was the "consciousness as of something forgotten," the "thrill of returning thought."

With the breakthrough to language not only are signals transformed into signs of reality, but reality itself is transformed, perhaps even for the first time formed. With this breakthrough Helen Keller moves from having an environment (*Umwelt*) to having a world (*Welt*) in which every object "quiver[s] with life." This reality is a human world, a moral universe. Helen Keller can feel now those truly human feelings of repentance and sorrow, and precisely because of that it is a world of human joy. It is a world of community—a world filled with mothers and fathers, sisters and brothers, teachers and students.

The example is enlightening because it highlights the role of the mediator as the namer. There is no breakthrough to language without a namer, without an intersubjective situation, a model who gives the name. In this instance the mediator, teacher Ann Sullivan, opens up a world. There is no rivalry over a desired object. The teacher is simply disclosing what water is, and Helen Keller becomes her co-celebrant in the joy of apprehending reality.

The experience of Helen Keller is unusual only because of her acute consciousness that a fundamental breakthrough had occurred, one most of us experience without a concomitant awareness of its astonishing implications. Still, the experience is not unknown to us. All of us probably can call to mind moments when something of which we had been vaguely aware gets put into words for us. This experience comes in a variety of settings—conversations with friends, in therapy, reading poetry or novels—but is always mediated to us by another. The other person expresses what you or I have been sensing without being able to articulate it. When we hear or read that articulation, we know that we are not alone, and we rejoice. It can be as profound an experience as Helen Keller's. It opens up whole dimensions of reality—undying love, ravishing beauty, inconsolable sorrow, even transcendence.

Now to the scandal, however. This is not the end of the story but only its beginning. Helen Keller entered a human world of joy and community, yet the child who fell asleep longing for a new day will wake up. She will be thirsty and ask for water. Will the word *water* always bring light, hope, joy, and freedom to her? On the following morning it might have a kind of afterglow, but that will gradually fade. Will the word continue to fill her with the "thrill of returning thought"? If we admit that language will not always bring her this kind of grace, it is not enough to think that this is due to the novelty having worn off. Some deeper problem manifests itself here.

The phenomenon is no less puzzling for being so familiar: words lose their meaning. They do not lose it in the sense that they lose their denotation. This is one of the hallmarks of language versus stimulus-response. Whereas Pavlov's dogs need to have the connection between bell and food continually reinforced, lest the response be extinguished, I can go fifty years without hearing the word or actually seeing an aardvark and still know what the word denotes. No, words lose their meaning in the sense that they lose their power to grant access to reality and instead become a block to that very reality. It becomes harder to say what we want because somehow the words are "used up."

Language not only loses its power, but it also gets corrupted. Words begin to carry the opposite meaning. This kind of transformation occurs when the model of what is desirable becomes the rival for the desirable object. Once a person begins to desire what the model desires, he learns very quickly that disclosing the desire—naming it, speaking it—is the shortest route to making certain that he will never obtain the object. In this situation only dissimulation will succeed, and the best way to dissimulate is to say the opposite of what one means.[9]

Then not only do words lose their meaning but reality itself loses its mysteriousness and depth. It becomes simultaneously dense, nugatory, and metaphysically weightless. When this happens, one has the opposite experience from Helen Keller's breakthrough. One feels that words simply occlude and obscure, that language lies and distorts. At the extreme end of this experience one wants no longer to speak or hear but only to withdraw into a silent world.[10]

How and why does this happen? We know that words can conceal as well as reveal, but how is it that the very thing that grants us access can also block reality? This is what I mean by scandal at the level of language.

Again Walker Percy suggests several ways of looking at this phenomenon. He begins by drawing our attention to the curious fact that, outside of language also, the very things that are meant to make a thing accessible (sometimes physically accessible) end up rendering it invisible or otherwise inaccessible. The way a reality gets "packaged" ends up drawing more attention to the packaging than to the reality. His example is the Grand Canyon. No longer do we have to trek through hundreds of miles of mesquite carrying all our supplies with us as García López de Cárdenas had to. We do not experience the ordeal, and thus we do not experience the joy of having the canyon open up before us. Cárdenas had no mediators and no rivals. In sharp contrast, we drive right up to the rim, get out, take a few pictures, and leave. Have we *seen* the Grand Canyon? The mediator for us is all the efforts of the National Park Service to make the canyon visible. However, these efforts can end up actually taking the canyon away, depriving us of our own experience and possibly triggering resentment.

The epistemological reason for this phenomenon is that human cognition gives priority to its own conceptual formation over the thing itself. The Grand Canyon itself is measured against everything I have ever heard or read about it. The idea here is not that it is better to approach the canyon with an "empty head" rather than knowing about its geological formations and history. The "empty head" approach leaves one even more bereft of experience.[11] The problem lies in another direction. Human knowing, instead of appreciating the Grand Canyon in its "suchness," compares it with its own conception as preformed by such things as precepts, words, and images of the canyon. The seemingly innocent saying "It's as pretty as a picture," uttered while surveying the Grand Canyon, reveals a massive epistemological reversal. The Grand Canyon has been photographed, painted, and filmed in order to represent its actuality, but now the actuality has to measure up to our image of it.

Beneath this epistemic reason is the social or interpersonal reason that grounds it. The concepts I have of the Grand Canyon did not arise in a vacuum. My experience is in competition with my friends' experiences; it is in competition with my fellow travelers' experiences. (Why do we despise and avoid other tourists? Why do people come back from a trip and, when asked "How was it?" reply "Great. There were no tourists"?) The role of the mediator is *never* absent, and the rivalry with the mediator is *seldom* absent.

To summarize: Helen Keller begins by learning that this cool, flowing liquid is the word "water." This vocable becomes water; it will substitute for any instantiation of the object. The word itself gets informed by the cool, flowing, cleansing, thirst-quenching reality that is water. As I said, it *becomes* water, and, therefore, it sounds more "watery" to an English speaker than "dust." Unfortunately, the process does not end there. As Percy observes, the word hardens around the signified so that "in the end the signified becomes encased in a simulacrum like a mummy in a mummy case."[12] A devaluation occurs. What previously revealed reality and made it accessible now swallows it up. Water, the liquid, disappears into the word "water." "The unique reality is assigned to its class of signs, a second-class mummy in the basement collection of mummy cases."[13] It becomes merely a particular instance of a more general concept, with the latter assuming priority.

It seems, then, that there is a duality and a duplicity built into language and its relation to reality. The way in which language informs reality is such that both are rendered deeply ambiguous and unstable. For words to lose their meaning implies that we, as language-users, also lose the reality to which they grant access. To lose the reality is no longer to have anything to talk about. But these kinds of losses are not simply privative experiences. A word's loss of meaning is not like a balloon's loss of air. We experience the word as positively blocking the reality that before it seemed to open up. And reality becomes not simply bland but unspeakable.

Percy's image of the word as a mummy case is not fortuitous. The signifier does indeed harden around the signified, yet Percy seems to suggest a possibility of recovering meaning by breaking open this hardened shell, as if the mummy were still alive. "A recovery is possible," he writes. "The signified can be recovered from an ossified signifier."[14] To an extent this is true. Using one of his own examples again, a person may ignore all the modern conveniences supplied by the National Park Service and hike to the Grand Canyon's rugged North Rim carrying her own supplies in order to have a more authentic experience of it. Such strategies do work but, as Percy acknowledges, they are no more than displacements of the underlying problem. Such strategies become immediately subject to the same dialectic of the decay of meaning. Initially they offer access, but then they end up blocking it. The strategy of "getting off the beaten path" becomes a beaten path and so on. This suggests that not only are the strategies scandalous in the sense I have defined the term—they both grant and deny access—but also that scandal itself now becomes one of the strategies for recovering meaning. Our fascination with scandal is precisely because it promises to make things interesting, more alive, more real, even if there is an ultimate letdown.

Percy's suggestion that one need only break open the hardened signifier, the "mummy," in order to release the living signified seems at first to indicate a certain incoherence in his choice of imagery. Inside a mummy's case is a corpse, not a living entity, but let us follow his suggestion. Language then becomes something analogous to the scene which Leontius came upon as he was going up from the Piraeus: a collection of corpses at the foot of the executioner. Only these corpses are in sarcophagi. Dare we open them? Like Leontius, we want both to look and not to look at the corpses, at the very generation of meaning and order.

We began with Danner's recommendation that we "look long and hard" at the victims of society's violence. We moved from there, through a consideration of the scandal involved in such looking, to reflections on language's simultaneous granting and blocking of access to reality. That discussion led us back to the victim because the metaphorical corpses in sarcophagi turned out to be real.

All the elements that I have introduced so far—the desire for and the shame of looking at violence, the presence of a mediator, scandal, rivalry, idolatry, and language—point in this direction, but the paradigm still seems far-fetched. The loss of meaning and the concomitant loss of reality suggest that the origin of language was itself something of a scandal, something that both opened up reality and occluded it. The ultimate reason why words lose their meaning and reality its density is that from the beginning, even before articulate language, the first signifier really was a corpse.

René Girard provides us with a way of understanding how this came about. According to him, such a system of signification came into being when "consciousness" became one person's consciousness of a victim as linked "structurally to the prodigious effects produced by [the victim's] passage from life to death, by the spectacular and liberating reversal that has occurred at that instant."[15] These "prodigious effects" are necessary because the primitive human community was threatened with extinction through its own violence. As the rivalries escalated into conflicts that spread, the danger of humanity vanishing before it established itself was real. The escape from this communal death was to substitute one member for all. Some mediator then designated one member of the community as responsible for the violence that threatened it. In this sacrificial moment of substitution occurred a "double transference" to the victim of all the evil that the community had been experiencing before his death and of all of the good that the community experienced afterward. This double transference could occur only under the auspices of a mediator. According to Girard, this is the "only possible meaning" and "constitute[s] the sacred."

> Because of the victim, in so far as it seems to emerge from the community and the community seems to emerge from it, for the first time there can be something like an inside and an outside, a before and after, a community and the sacred. We have already noted that the victim appears to be simultaneously good and evil, peaceable and violent, a life that brings death and a death that guarantees life. Every possible significant element seems to have its outline in the sacred and at the same time to be transcended by it. In this sense the victim does seem to constitute a universal signifier. (*TH*, 102)

The victim, then, is not a signified trapped within a mummified signifier. What is within the mummy case does not hold the final thing that we are seeking, although it does lead us in this direction. It seduces us into supposing that, if we can just break through the last signifier, we will find the ultimate or "transcendental" signified. But no. The victim, that which is in the mummified signifier, is itself the sacred *signifier*. "The signifier is the victim," writes Girard. "The signified constitutes all actual and potential meaning the community confers on the victim, and through its intermediacy, on to all things" (*TH*, 102).

The signifier stands in the place of both horrible violence and miraculous peace because it stands in the place of or substitutes for the community. We will see throughout this work how authors use substitutions to both mesmerize and to reveal. Here it would seem that we have a single signifier with a double significance, but this is to ignore the way in which signifier and signified inform each other. The victim is the *signifier*, and, since the signified is dual, so is the signifier also necessarily dual—both revelatory and obfuscating, granting access to reality and blocking it. The first signifier is scandalous and underneath that scandal is all of the rivalry that led to the victim's climactic demise.

The signifier signifies something as both bad and good, malevolent and benevolent, because that is the way it is experienced. In this sense the signifier is true. The reality it signifies, however, is one that is the result of an arbitrary choice on the part of a mediator who indicates the victim and then of the community that projects all evil and then all good onto him or her. In this sense the signifier is also a lie. He or she is an innocent victim who is held to be guilty of all the evil but who now becomes the source of all blessing. The evil and the blessings are real, but the victim's guilt and beneficence are not true. Thus the transcendental signifier is a fundamental misrecognition of the truth. Its representation in language shares in this duplicity.

The victim is *the* symbolic office. The victim represents not himself but all of the problems, all of the evil, that the community transfers to him. He also represents all of the blessings that flow from the peace that results from his killing. The victim as signifier holds out the possibility of peace, but only by means of violence. He grants access to peace and reconciliation by also blocking that very peace and reconciliation for at least one member of the community: himself.

Destruction of a bearer of meaning (the signifier) in order to release its meaning (the signified) is grounded in this ancient, sacrificial view of meaning: the destruction of the victim brings blessings from the gods. The victim, whose death reconciles the community with the gods and each other, is the universal signifier of violence and peace, life and death. Violence becomes a method for generating significance even in the modern world. We see this when the reaction to the scandal that something is being hidden or withheld by the cultural signifier that promised access leads to the destruction of the signifier in the hope of releasing meaning. (Recall Percy's image of the pristine object trapped in the mummy case.) The signifier (victim) is already a scandal, someone in whose being the others see both promised access to blessings and blocked access to those blessings. It can appear that only the destruction of the victim will release what the others desire.

The process works. When the victim is destroyed, the blessings of peace come, but the victim was not responsible for the community's ills, and so they are not really healed. Instead, they begin to fester and spread again, until another sacrifice is required. Language mediates a signifier as a substitute for sacrifice. This is the lie.

No one understood the duality and duplicity of language as well as Friedrich Nietzsche. In fact, as we shall see in the next chapter, this duplicity is the key to his understanding of the origin of Greek tragedy and, thus, Western culture. In *The Birth of Tragedy: Out of the Spirit of Music*, Nietzsche explains that the origin of tragedy was sacrifice.[16] In this context sacrifice was a spectacle that seemed to grant access to a deeper reality but, in fact, kept one from seeing the truth. This return to a sacred origin would be his way to renew not only the study of tragedy but contemporary culture as well. I will show that this was a false promise.

CHAPTER 2

The Fascination of Friedrich Nietzsche

To Look and To Go Beyond Mere Looking

We began with Leontius going up from the Pireaus. In his encounter with the corpses he was aware of three things: that he wanted to look at the executed corpses, that he did not want to look, and that neither the looking nor the not looking would leave him fully satisfied. He was seemingly unaware of the executioner, whom he saw but did not address. The scandalous nature of Leontius's struggle, consisting of both an explicit struggle with his desires to look and not to look on the victims and an implicit rivalry with the executioner, is not rare. Even if we do not come across victims of violence, we all engage, under the cover of the struggle to know and to keep ourselves from knowing, in a struggle with the mediator. Most of the time we choose to concentrate on the former struggle and pretend that the latter does not exist. But it is the latter, and not the former, struggle that defines who we are. It also determines what we will see when we do look at the victim.

In the context of rivalry we begin to dissimulate, to say the opposite of what we mean, to deceive in order to get the better of our rival. Words begin to lose their meaning and to occlude reality as we try to build an order on

20   Chapter 2

the sarcophagi of dead victims. Thus, at the root of this phenomenon is our relationship to the mediator and, by extension, to the victim.

I turn to Friedrich Nietzsche and his *The Birth of Tragedy Out of the Spirit of Music* because I am convinced that understanding the origin of the phenomenon gives us a better understanding of ourselves.[1] Our present consciousness constitutes and is constituted by our understanding of origins, such that a deepening of the one results in a deepening of the other. *The Birth of Tragedy* is a perfect example of the phenomenon we seek to understand. Nietzsche, like Leontius, wants to look and resists looking at the victims of violence, all the while pretending that the mediator is not there. Nietzsche fascinates the eye of the reader's mind with the spectacle of describing the fascination of the eye of the body.

Nietzsche is valuable because he is the master of doing precisely what we are trying to explore—drawing the reader in yet not letting her see, saying things in such a beautiful manner that one forgets the sordid reality about which he is actually speaking. He makes one want to be beyond knowing. That is both his genius and his danger. Nietzsche's work gives us a chance to experience how the truth of violence gets expelled from a text and, in being expelled, forms the text. Specifically, in *The Birth of Tragedy* he is intent on expelling the ancient Greek playwright Euripides. Relying on Girard's interpretation of Euripides's *The Bacchae*, I make clear that Nietzsche is trying to get rid of that which might allow us to see the victim at the heart of tragedy.

At the same time Nietzsche helps us to see how inaccurate it is to describe Leontius's situation as simply involving a conflict between two desires, one positive and the other negative. He demonstrates that something more profound is going on here than our usual calculus of benefit and harm in pursuing or not pursuing a particular action. According to Nietzsche, a dual and duplicitous desire, consisting in both wanting to look and wanting to go beyond mere looking, better captures the reality.

The person who is both attracted and repelled—that is, scandalized—wants to transcend the situation. She is aware that neither giving in and looking nor avoiding the sight is going to satisfy. To answer her need for transcendence, Nietzsche calls for art, which he identifies with religion and myth. According to him, the art she is seeking is the tragic art of ancient Greece, which in its purest moments consisted in transforming the spectator into a satyr through the mediation of the chorus. The transformed spectator could then look upon the dismemberment of Dionysus with joy because of the beautiful Apollonian illusion of it all. Nietzsche's *The Birth of Tragedy* inscribes this theory by attempting to transform the reader into a satyr, a votary of Dionysus, so that he or she can look upon the represented murder of Socrates, the theoretical man, with joy.

To return to the story of Leontius, tragedy should make it possible for him to look not "long and hard," as Danner recommends, but in a more aesthetic way by covering the corpses with a beautiful illusion. In effect, tragedy does this by making the spectator one with the executioner in leading us beyond what Nietzsche calls "the utter delight in appearance" and searching for the even "higher satisfaction from the destruction of the visible world of appearance" (114). However, making the spectator one with the executioner is not done in the service of raising the spectator's consciousness of the presence of the mediator. Quite to the contrary, Nietzsche's text is about the struggle to see and be beyond seeing, and it suppresses the mediator's presence and rivalry that makes this desire so strong.

Nietzsche's analysis in *The Birth of Tragedy* is concerned overtly with the fascination of the individual's destruction, but it is covertly about rivalry. Such rivalry with the model/mediator appears most clearly in the "Preface to Richard Wagner," in response to whose "real presence" the whole book was written. Wagner was also Nietzsche's "noble champion" on the path of art as the supreme task and metaphysical activity (13). To say, somewhat abstractly, that Nietzsche wanted his readers to become votaries of Dionysus is to suggest that he wanted them to become votaries of Wagner. It is well known that Nietzsche's admiration of Wagner later turned into hatred and that eventually Nietzsche hoped that the regard people had for Wagner would be directed toward himself. Girard's words are apropos here:

> The mediator is the real center around which everything revolves in proportion to the madman's desire to have everything revolve around himself. As a result, the text must be generated by desire itself. The absence of the mediator is the surest clue to his continued omnipotence, the infallible sign that the fires of mediation will go on burning higher and higher.[2]

Nietzsche was not yet a "madman" when he wrote *The Birth of Tragedy*, but the lines that will converge into his later madness are already present in this work of genius. Nietzsche and his first text take us back to the origin, both in terms of Western culture and in terms of the individual Nietzsche, to the source of madness.

Nietzsche was trying to draw a scandalized reaction from people and even at this early stage, in addition to his adulation of Wagner, he sees himself in rivalry with the Judeo-Christian tradition. The work itself is scandalous in that it is deliberately "monstrous" or a combination of two heterogeneous genres: theoretical aesthetics and tragic drama. While Nietzsche endeavors to turn the human gaze from ephemeral reality back to an unveiling of truth, he leads the reader not to look at the truth but rather to return to the primitive fascination of continual unveiling.

A Scandalous Work

Nietzsche knew, even as he published it, that *The Birth of Tragedy* would not be accepted by other scholars in his field. He wrote to his own teacher after not hearing anything for more than a month after its publication, "The book, after all, is something of a manifesto, and the last thing it invites is silence."[3] Like most manifestoes, *The Birth of Tragedy* was meant to originate a movement. Nietzsche thus writes: "Let us imagine a rising generation with such an undaunted gaze, with such a heroic proclivity for the tremendous. Let us imagine the bold stride of those dragon-slayers, the proud audacity with which they turn their backs on all the weaklings' doctrines that lie within that optimism, in order to 'live resolutely' in all that they do" (88). Such is the kind of movement he hoped to found.

What his treatise almost immediately inspired, however, was not a following but rather a scathing attack from another scholar, Ulrich von Wilamowitz-Moellendorff, titled *Zukunftsphilologie* [*Philology for the Future*]. While this may not have been what Nietzsche hoped for, it was much better than silence. He desired either passionate acceptance or passionate rejection because, as I will try to show, in the end they both accomplish his purpose.

Nietzsche was in rivalry with more than Wagner. In his "Attempt at Self-Criticism" (added 15 years later, it contains Nietzsche's reflections on *The Birth of Tragedy*), he admits that his work treats Christianity with a "discreet and hostile silence." At the same time, he avers that "nothing could be more opposed to the purely aesthetic interpretation and justification of the world as taught in this book than Christian doctrine" (8). Christianity is thus the target against which the work is directed in its attempt to resurrect Dionysian culture, but Nietzsche could not make this rivalry explicit.

He does, however, make an exception to his "hostile silence." At one point in the text Nietzsche compares the Aryan myth of Prometheus with the Semitic myth of the Fall. There is an interplay here of various rivalries: the rivalry between modernity and the ancients, the rivalry between different national expropriations of the Greek legacy, the rivalry between Athens and Jerusalem, the rivalry between male and female, as well as the explicit rivalry between the "Aryan" and the "Semitic."

Both Prometheus's theft of fire and Eve's disobedience in eating the forbidden fruit present the "insoluble contradiction between man and the gods." This contradiction is the "first philosophical problem" as well as a religious problem. The contradictory relationship between the human and the transcendent lies "like a boulder at the gates of every culture" (49). For Nietzsche, then, at the very place one hopes to enter into an understanding of culture, one is confronted with an insoluble contradiction, a stumbling block; in other words, a scandal. The place of promised access is blocked.

According to Nietzsche, "to plumb the full depths of [the myth of Prometheus's] terrors" is to see as its premise "the supreme value that primitive man places on *fire* as the true palladium of any rising culture" (49). Nevertheless, primitive man can conceive of having complete responsibility for fire as a sacrilege, an offense against the gods. Primitive man develops a distorted vision according to which, because of the control that he has "plundered" or wrested from the gods, he suffers violence from the offended deities. This contestation creates the "first philosophical problem": humankind's violent relationship to transcendence. It is a struggle between man and the gods, which is ultimately the contradiction of violence. As long as a person has taken something away from someone else, the danger remains that someone else will take it away. The original thief or violator is never secure, never at peace. She remains in conflict with reality. For Nietzsche this problem situates the conflictual relationship between God and man. It becomes the problem of violence and the sacred as a portal to culture.

The Question of Genre

For Nietzsche there is no way of transcending the conflict between the human and the transcendent. Rather, one must eternally repeat the struggle; one lives a scandalized existence. This eternal recurrence gets written into the text of *The Birth of Tragedy*. Tragedy is not born once. It is born, dies, or, more accurately, is killed before being born anew. Part of the greatness of Nietzsche's text is its ability to scandalize each new generation of readers.

As we read *The Birth of Tragedy* with a view to avoiding scandal, one question is important: what kind of writing is this? What has disturbed not only other commentators but also Nietzsche himself is the dual nature of the work.[4] *The Birth of Tragedy* is a theory about tragedy—that is, it is a scholarly contribution to aesthetics. It thus is *Wissenschaft* (science), but Nietzsche's theoretical understanding of aesthetics demands that any true theory of tragedy be non-theoretical or practical. Aesthetics must be a practical art; it must teach humans how to live because, once again, it is meant to replace religion in general and Christianity in particular. It cannot be practical as a theory but only as an art. *The Birth of Tragedy* overcomes the distinction between theory and practice by overcoming the distinction between science (*Wissenschaft*) and art (*Kunst*). It overcomes it by practicing its theory in the text. *The Birth of Tragedy* is itself not simply about tragedy; it is itself a tragedy in that it attempts to produce and not just describe the "tragic effect" in the reader, so that tragedy might be born again.[5] A work that transgresses traditional boundaries is often called scandalous. *The Birth of Tragedy* is a "monstrous," genre-bending work, and so scandalous. It is only when the text is read in this way that one can fully comprehend it.

Science and Art

The reader needs to understand why this manner of writing is the only one that conforms to Nietzsche's aesthetic theory. He was aware that by writing in this way he transformed not only the science of aesthetics into a practical art but, in so doing, also hoped to transform art itself. He wanted aesthetics to become both theoretical and practical, while art would become at once a practical and a theoretical enterprise.

The crossing of categories that Nietzsche undertook consisted in the bold attempt to transform aesthetics from being simply the science of beauty—a disinterested description of how certain cultural artifacts such as tragedy achieve their effects—into being the practice of justifying human existence when conceived as an "aesthetic phenomenon." Justifying human existence was to be the end or purpose of art in general and of tragedy in particular.[6] The new science of aesthetics was to make this end manifest and, in a certain sense, to take it over. Aesthetics would then have an extremely practical bent: it would give humans a reason for living; it would justify human existence in the face of the pain and horror of life. We could say that it would paradoxically allow Leontius to gaze at the corpses by casting a veil over them.

Aesthetics was to have as its purpose an understanding of this justification of life by art, but it could not do this simply as theory. In fact, this purpose had been historically frustrated by the theoretical attitude embodied in Socrates that Nietzsche identifies with Alexandrian culture. In order for aesthetics to cease being a block, Nietzsche had to rewrite aesthetics in such a way that it would lead the modern reader to the same insight to which tragedy led the Greeks. This art form was for Nietzsche the exemplar of all art. Tragedy made it possible for humans to live. Thus, aesthetics, and so in turn *The Birth of Tragedy* itself, could not merely theorize about tragedy but had to embody it. It is only in reading his text as doubling back upon itself, in the sense that the theory also inscribes a praxis, that its meaning begins to unfold. Our usual distinctions between theory and praxis, as well as those between science, art, and religion, do not apply here. In *The Birth of Tragedy* Nietzsche was attempting to undo the distinction between art and philosophy, thus rendering his text a religious work because the justification of human existence by the new practical science of aesthetics would not be merely art but also a kind of religion. His inaugural work enacted tragedy so that humans would not have to live by relying on traditional religion. Nietzsche wanted us to return to pagan religion through an experience of its art.

Such a return to religion under the guise of art is important because it makes explicit what Nietzsche leaves unsaid. Girard puts it this way:

Religion, then, is far from 'useless.' It dehumanizes violence; it protects man from his own violence by taking it out of his hands, transforming it into a transcendent and ever-present danger to be kept in check by appropriate rites appropriately observed and by a modest and prudent demeanor. Religious misinterpretation is a truly constructive force, for it purges man of the suspicions that would poison his existence if he were to remain conscious of the crisis as it actually took place.[7]

Nietzsche, for his part, sees the effect of the god Apollo as that which allows deception concerning the "universality of the Dionysian event" (102). The very pity that tragedy stirs in the spectator "deliver[s] us from the primal suffering of the world, just as the symbol of the myth preserves us from gazing directly on the supreme idea of the world, just as thoughts and words save us from the unbrooked effusion of the unconscious will" (102). The "supreme idea of the world," the "unbrooked effusion of the unconscious will," is violence.

The Tragic Effect

Perhaps the best way to grasp what the essence of tragedy was for Nietzsche is to listen to his description of what Euripides experienced when he watched Aeschylean, or earlier and truer, tragedy. In the theatre Euripides experienced something "which anyone initiated into the deeper secrets of Aeschylean tragedy might have foretold":

> In every feature, every line, he found something incommensurable, a certain deceptive precision and at the same time an enigmatic depth, an infinite background. The clearest character still had a comet's tail attached to it, which seemed to point to uncertainty, to something that could not be illuminated. The same twilight (*Zwielicht*) shrouded the structure of the play, particularly the meaning of the chorus. (58–59)

We see here quite clearly the dual nature that is the essence of tragedy. Certainly something is revealed, but what is revealed is that something is hidden. There is "something incommensurable" in every line. Thus, the essence of tragedy is such that what is revealed is an *Umschleirung*,[8] a veiling. More than that, that which is revealed as hidden seems to invite further investigation; it seems to promise to reveal itself, yet it never does. That something leads the spectator or thinker on, always further on, but never satisfies.

Later in the work Nietzsche also gives a kind of phenomenology of the "effect of true musical tragedy" so that the "attentive friend" can "interpret his own experiences" (105). As the tragic myth is presented, he feels "a kind of omniscience, as if his powers of vision were not merely superficial but could penetrate to the very depths" (105). The world is "transfigured," but it is precisely this world that is also denied (105). This denial is not some flight into unreality but precisely the viewer's "rejoicing" in the "destruction" of the tragic hero. The viewer comprehends the tragic events "to their very depths," yet he loves to "escape into incomprehension" (105). We have the juxtaposition of an apparently omniscient view that ends in incomprehension. Nietzsche's formulates this most clearly when he writes: "He looks more keenly, more deeply than ever, and yet wishes for blindness" (105). This does not mean that one does, in fact, see everything and only wishes to be blind. In the drama one penetrates into the inner world, yet "we felt as though we were watching a symbol, almost imagining we could divine its deepest meaning, and wishing to draw it aside like a curtain to glimpse the primordial image that lay behind" (113). With tragedy there always remains something more deeply hidden, no matter how much has been unveiled, no matter how deeply our sight penetrates. The clarity of the picture does not satisfy. The effect on the viewer is clear: the eye is kept "in thrall" but cannot penetrate further

> for [the image] seemed to reveal as much as it concealed; and while it seemed, with its symbolic revelation, to demand that we tear the veil, that we reveal the mysteries behind it, that brightly lit clarity kept the eye in thrall and resisted further penetration. (113)

For Nietzsche, then, tragedy is that which compels us to look but never allows us to see. It is literally the story of the violent death of an innocent victim told in such a way that the victim's innocence remains hidden and the violence is justified. Tragedy is the story of the myth of Dionysus. It is a story of revenge. Dionysus wants revenge on those who have refused him worship.

It is also a repetition. Dionysus arranges that what has already happened to himself, namely his dismemberment by the Titans, happens to Pentheus. It is also a story of seduction. Dionysus succeeds in driving Pentheus mad, fascinating him with that which at first repelled him. Dionysus gets Pentheus to look voyeuristically on the Maenads or female worshippers of Dionysus. The Maenads are in an insane frenzy when Pentheus sees them. They spot him and, mistaking him for a wild animal, dismember him with their bare hands. His mother is one of the Maenads, and she leads the way in the killing. The women are exiled from Thebes, and thus Dionysus's revenge is exacted.

Like Pentheus, we want to look at the sacred mysteries of this orgiastic cult, but these mysteries are so constructed that they distract us from their reality. To see the reality, we would have to get beneath the surface, but tragedy is designed (at least before the appearance of Euripides) to *prevent* that. It keeps the viewer in subjugation without ever revealing the real mystery. The viewing itself becomes the reason why one cannot see. For Nietzsche the real mystery here is not tragedy but the "marvelous schism within the self" that allows for tragedy, for wanting to see and wanting to be beyond seeing, to exist (105).

The particular aesthetic experience of the split self for the spectator of tragedy is the clue that Nietzsche needs to reconstruct the genesis of the tragic myth because some kind of analogous experience goes on inside the tragic artist to produce the myth. The artist first combines the delight in creating images with the higher delight in destroying the visible world. This higher pleasure is the "destruction" of the "the whole world of phenomenon" (106). All of this depends upon the surrogate victim without whom "men would not be able to shake loose the violence between them, to make of it a separate entity both sovereign and redemptory."[9] Violence has the last word and imposes its meaning, yet that meaning is hidden and has to be hidden in order to be effective. "For religion," writes Girard, "protects man as long as its ultimate foundations are not revealed."[10] This leads to two different end points—an aesthetic in Nietzsche that is conscious of its untruth and a revelation in Girard that reveals the misrecognition. "In fact, the sacrificial crisis is simply another form of that knowledge which grows greater as the reciprocal violence grows more intense but which never leads to the whole truth. It is the knowledge of violence, along with the violence itself, that the act of expulsion succeeds in shunting outside the realm of consciousness."[11]

To grasp the significance of this mystery, Nietzsche turns to a musical analogue. He states that "we might characterize this condition with reference to artistically applied dissonance, by saying that we want to hear and long to go beyond hearing" (115). As I stated above, this longing to be "beyond seeing" or "go beyond hearing" is a longing for transcendence. For Nietzsche, following in the footsteps of Heraclitus, this transcendence is violence. Nietzsche often phrases it to mean that the "world of the individual" is playfully destroyed, like a child's knocking down the sandcastles that he or she has built upon the shore, but this kind of phrasing and image is Nietzsche's own Apollonian attempt to hold the reader's eye enthralled. Such enthrallment Nietzsche calls, in another passage, the "supreme and properly serious task of art" (93–94). Art entails "rescuing the eye from gazing into the horrors of night and releasing the subject, with the healing balm of illusion, from the convulsive stirrings of the will" (94). The tragic artist does this in creating the tragic myth (114). Let us apply this process to *The Birth of Tragedy* itself in order to substantiate my claim that Nietzsche is writing tragedy.

How Tragedy is Effected in *The Birth of Tragedy*

In order to show fully the process by which Nietzsche brings about the tragic effect in *The Birth of Tragedy*, we have to begin with the very first sentence that contains the famous conception of art as the balance of the Apollonian and the Dionysian:

> We shall have gained much for the science of aesthetics when we have the unmediated certainty of intuition, and not just the logical insight, that continuous development of art depend upon the duality [*die Duplicität*] of the *Apollonian* and *Dionysian*. . . . (14)

We must give this sentence a new interpretation. The duality that is a duplicity is not, according to our view, the duality *between* Apollo and Dionysus but before all else *within* the Apollonian and the Dionysian respectively. As Girard comments in *Violence and the Sacred*, "(A parenthetic remark on Nietzsche: although his classifications [the Apollonian and the Dionysian] are manifestly superior to the approaches of most critics, they fail to perceive, or at most perceive only dimly, that each and every divinity corresponds to both aspects at once)."[12] In *The Birth of Tragedy* every distinction asserted by Nietzsche, including this most famous one between Apollo and Dionysus, is at the same time denied, and denied not through oversight or lack of consistency but deliberately because Nietzsche is adhering to the logic of the tragic, a logic that expresses the "contradiction in the heart of the world."[13]

The Birth of Tragedy contains what Nietzsche himself identifies as the "content of the tragic myth"—namely, "an epic event that glorifies the struggling hero" (114). It is precisely in the reader's rejoicing in the annihilation of the hero that the tragic effect is achieved. It is in seeing a new order emerge from the death of the old that the aesthetic experience of tragedy consists.

All of the elements enumerated so far are important: the gaze that is held in thrall by that from which it would fain turn away, the joy at the annihilation of a person, and the emergence of a new order. These elements suggest what will eventually be made explicit: tragedy's power is rooted in sacrifice.[14]

The tragic hero of *The Birth of Tragedy* is not Greek tragedy itself, although its death is also recorded. Because Greek tragedy is too far removed from the modern reader, he cannot identify himself with it and therefore cannot perceive its death as tragic. The tragic hero instead is Socrates as a symbolic or representative figure: "If we wish to consider Socrates as one of these charioteers of our own and all other cultures, we need only see him as the prototype of a new and unimagined life-form, the prototype of *theoretical man*" (72). Nietzsche thus explains the influence of Socrates, which extends to Nietzsche's own time and indeed "beyond" (71). This theoretical man is the true hero of the piece. The theoretical man in today's world is every man, every woman. All of us are the descendants of this Socrates; all of us are denizens of Alexandrian culture. At the same time, the theoretical man is no one particular person. Nietzsche thus performs an act of sacrificial substitution. First, almost unnoticed, Socrates is substituted for Euripides. Then the "figure" of Socrates is substituted for the historical person, and finally the "theoretical man" is substituted for that figure. It is no wonder that we get caught in the fascinating interplay of sacrificial substitutions.

Let us listen to Nietzsche's description of the struggle between Socrates and Dionysus in order to identify the main elements of this tragedy.

But Socrates was that *second spectator* who did not understand the older tragedy and therefore chose to ignore it; in league with him, Euripides dared to become the herald of a new creativity. If it was this that destroyed the older tragedy, then aesthetic Socratism is the principle behind its death [*das mörderische Prinzip*]. But in so far as the battle was directed against the Dionysian elements of the older part, we may call Socrates the opponent of Dionysus, the new Orpheus who rose up against Dionysus and, although destined to be torn to pieces by the Maenads of the Athenian court, put the powerful god to flight. The god, as when he fled Lycurgus, king of the Edoni, escaped into the depth of the sea, the mystical floods of a secret cult that was gradually to cover the whole world. (64)

We see in this quotation the basic pattern that allows the tragic insight to emerge. Socrates is both identified with and distinguished from Euripides. Socrates, then, opposes Dionysus; he struggles against him. Socrates or reason or the theoretical man—they are all equivalent—cannot comprehend, however, the irrational. He can only expel Dionysus and define himself and rationality over against Dionysus and the irrational. At the same time, Socrates is structurally identified with Dionysus. That is, exactly like Dionysus, Socrates is "destined to be torn to pieces by the Maenads of the Athenian court."[15] In expelling Dionysus, Socrates is not accomplishing anything definitive; he is only preparing the way for his own expulsion. Further, his expulsion of Dionysus serves to ensure the return of Dionysus. Dionysus simply hides himself in the "the mystical floods of a secret cult that was gradually to cover the whole world."

We can examine this pattern in a bit more detail. How exactly does Socrates oppose Dionysus? What forms does the opposition take? How does Dionysus work his return? Finally, we need to the raise the question of this troubling identification between the figure of Socrates and the figure of Dionysus.

Nietzsche tells us that Greek tragedy, unlike all the older sister arts, "died tragically by her own hand in consequence of an irreconcilable conflict" (54). It was originally Euripides who fought this death-struggle of tragedy. For Nietzsche, however, Euripides is "merely a mask" for Socrates (60). Euripides fought and vanquished Aeschylean tragedy with what Nietzsche calls a "*Socratic* intention," a tendency that precedes the historical Socrates (60). We can specify this intention: "The excision of the primitive and powerful Dionysian element from tragedy, and the rebuilding of tragedy on non-Dionysian art, morality and philosophy—this is the intention of Euripides, now revealed to us as clear as day" (59).

Although Nietzsche says, as quoted above, that tragedy died by her own hand, he blames Euripides for hounding Dionysus from the stage, for creating the "new opposition: the Dionysian and the Socratic, and that conflict was to be the downfall of Greek tragedy" (60). For Socrates, but Nietzsche equally means for Euripides, the tragic art never even appears "'to tell what's true'" (68). Therefore it must be rejected. For Euripides as well as Socrates, "in order to be beautiful, everything must be conscious" (64). Nietzsche is claiming that Socrates, and after him the whole philosophic tradition, made no attempt to get to the heart of tragedy, which is the beauty of the unintelligible or, more precisely, the making beautiful of that which we refuse to understand—the violent sacred. Instead, Socrates and the tradition rejected tragedy, fought against it, and expelled it. It might seem that rejecting the aestheticizing of what we refuse to understand is a step toward the truth, but in rejecting tragedy philosophy rejected the means by which it could have had access to the reality that tragedy represents. As Girard writes of Euripides's *The Bacchae*, "The tragic demystification discloses a bacchanal that is pure frenzy, naked violence."[16]

The Bacchae presents us with a rite that Euripides seems both to support and to abhor. According to Girard, Euripides had not, in fact, "fully acceded to the violent origin of the rite, the playing out of violence[,] and had [not fully] acknowledged the generative act of unanimity preserved by the rite, lost in the onslaught of reciprocal violence and recovered through the mechanism of the surrogate victim."[17] Had he done this, Euripides could have shown how both the good and the bad aspects, both the generating of the community and its destruction, have a common root in the sacrificial mechanism. Still, to his credit, Euripides does not adopt the attitude of primitive religion: he could have simply put the responsibility for the violence on the gods and absolved humans. He did neither, but he also did not back away from the crucial insight in silence. Euripides makes explicit the "poet's decision to retreat," and he offers justification.[18] Girard interprets him as speaking of "transgressing limits, of the fearsome knowledge that exists beyond these limits."[19]

Fearsome knowledge of what? The question is left hanging by Euripides. He gives us our world: an impious revolt against the gods, the division of the gods' followers into true believers and heretics, and, most importantly, a dual and duplicitous "enthusiasm," rewarded as a prize to the faithful and meted out as a punishment to the wicked. At the same time, this "Manichaean division between good and evil is no sooner proposed than it vanishes from sight."[20] The only way to resolve this tension would be to "establish a system of differentiation that did not dissolve under scrutiny and that permitted us to affirm the play's literary, psychological, and moral coherence. Such a system would be based, once again, on recourse to *arbitrary violence*."[21]

Nietzsche will not or cannot resolve this problem in this way. One reads Nietzsche with a sense that he knows he is talking about arbitrary violence, but he never quite admits as much. There is "primal oneness" and "destruction of the visible world of appearance," but what is actually meant is sordid: killing innocent victims. Only if Nietzsche embraces this violence does his nearly incredible claim to be the first to present a coherent theory of tragedy make any sense.

We have, then, a new antithesis—no longer the Apollonian and the Dionysian but "the Dionysian and the Socratic, and that conflict was to be the downfall of Greek tragedy" (60). Socrates expels Dionysian pessimism by means of theoretical optimism. This optimism consists in the threefold belief that "Virtue is knowledge[;] all sins arise from ignorance[;] the virtuous man is the happy man" (69). These positions are not unfamiliar, but what is unfamiliar is the genealogy that Nietzsche gives them. They do not stem, according to Nietzsche, from any Platonic insight into the Good; instead, they stem from a turning away from the deeper truth of Dionysus and from the attempt to expel it. Philosophy is a form of sacrifice: it sacrifices the truth hidden in Greek tragedy. Optimism is the weapon Socrates uses to expel the Dionysian.

Socrates succeeds in his struggle against the Dionysian. For a while at least he is able to make "existence appear intelligible and consequently justified" (73). What follows from Socrates is the whole history of philosophy in its widest sense—that is, the story of knowledge and its development. "Waves of philosophical schools emerged and vanished one after the other," comments Nietzsche (73). In this way Socrates becomes the turning point in the vortex of world history. Nietzsche feels that, if the force of Socratic optimism had not been there to harness the energies that it did, a practical pessimism—that is, life without the aesthetic justification it requires—could have led to "a terrible ethic of genocide through pity" (74). Art in the form of science or religion prevents this "breath of pestilence" (74). Nietzsche finally makes explicit here the connection I pointed out above between science, art, and religion. "If he [the theoretical man] sees here, to his dismay, how logic twists around itself and finally bites itself in the tail, there dawns a new form of knowledge, *tragic knowledge*, which needs art as both protection and remedy if we are to bear it" (75).

The wide ocean of knowledge onto which Socrates launched Western civilization has a paradoxical effect. That is, modern man sees the "limits" of this Socratic love of wisdom in its limitlessness and therefore searches for a coast in this ocean. It is precisely the limitlessness of the search that teaches modern man its limits. The limitlessness of Socrates is another form of optimism, an optimism founded on the delusion of limitless power (70–71).

It is not just society that suffers from internal contradictions. Science, and the culture that sustains it, only works so long as it has universal claims, but these claims get undercut through analysis of the limits of knowledge. This is the nature of "breach" in modern culture, the anxiety so many feel, when "theoretical man takes fright at his consequences" (88), yet "at the same time he feels how a culture based on the principle of science must perish once it begins to become *illogical*, to flee its own consequences" (89). It is Nietzsche's artistic philosophy or philosophic art that reveals in a universal manner the undoing of science's universal claims.

The Scandal

What has Nietzsche accomplished by his "art," which is also a theory of art? Nietzsche has, on the one hand, silently removed Euripides and, on the other, shown how Socrates, considered as the prototype of the theoretical man, as well as the philosophical tradition, are rooted in an expulsion of the irrational forces of Dionysus. He also has shown, very briefly but also brilliantly, how this expulsion ensures the return of that which is expelled. The culture built on logic becomes illogical and thus is led to the tragic insight, opening a way to the rebirth of tragedy. This is the historical moment at which Nietzsche finds himself.

If one follows the argument, one sees that Nietzsche has very skillfully led the reader to the following scandalous position: (1) one can accept Nietzsche's position, which is basically a rejection of Socrates, and follow Nietzsche's invitation at the work's end to "sacrifice" in the temples of Dionysus and Apollo; or (2) one can reject Nietzsche's analysis and side with Socrates. The choice, however, is not a choice, for to side with Socrates is still to side with the rejection of Dionysus and thus to ensure the return of Dionysus. Thus one's choice is between Dionysus or Dionysus. Socrates and the culture he represents become a 2000-year detour that comes back to the ineffable, the arbitrary violence, from which it began.

Another way of putting this is that Nietzsche has so framed *The Birth of Tragedy* that the reader can be scandalized at Socrates as the murderer of Greek tragedy, or at Dionysus as the scandal of reason, or at Nietzsche for pointing these things out. What one cannot be is *not* scandalized. One can be enthralled by any number of things in this fascinating text. One begins to long to understand and to be beyond understanding. The text itself, however, will not let you go.

The way through scandal to a deeper understanding involves exploring the silent expulsion of Euripides as well as the exact nature of the identity, asserted by Nietzsche, between Socrates and Dionysus. Is this simply an arbitrary identification made by Nietzsche at the beginning of his argument to ensure that it would end there? I do not think so. We must understand upon what the assertion of their identity is based. It is based on the fact that both Socrates and Dionysus are the victims of violence.

Socrates is the victim of political violence. We are back to Manigat's observation quoted at the beginning of this book: just staring at the corpse leads us nowhere, but "through the portal of political violence" lies an understanding of "the real workings of a society." We have to resist letting the "*dying Socrates*" become a "new ideal" because that way, according to Nietzsche, lies the idolatry of Plato, who "prostrated himself before the image with all the fervent devotion of a fanatic soul" (67). The figure of Socrates lends itself to the kind of fascinated gaze that does not differ in kind from that elicited by Aeschylean tragedy. We will not free ourselves from scandal through idolatry.

In fact, the idolatry of Plato provides one of the forces behind the development of art in the Western world. The figure of Socrates is something that can enthrall the eye in a way that makes him the equivalent of Dionysus. Nietzsche makes his real contribution to our project here because he shows that in expelling tragedy Socrates, and through him Plato, guarantees the return of the tragic. The rejection of tragedy causes Plato to "force poetry itself into new and unknown channels." In fact, he had to create a new form of art that "was related on a deep level to the art forms already in existence." Plato accused the older art forms of being the "counterfeit of an illusion" (68). To avoid that accusation himself, Plato had to try to go beyond reality, to make the reader want to see and, at the same time, long to be beyond seeing. Asserts Nietzsche:

> But in the process Plato the thinker had taken a detour to arrive at a place where Plato the poet had always been at home—a place from which Sophocles and the whole of the older arts solemnly protested against any accusations. If tragedy had absorbed all earlier genres within itself, the same might be said, in an eccentric sense, of the Platonic dialogue. (68)

Nietzsche's formulation is crucial. The Platonic dialogue is a place from which Plato and the philosophic tradition can protest against accusations. It is a defensive position that says, in effect, "We were not the ones who killed Socrates. We are innocent of that accusation." On the one hand, it seems to put philosophy on the side of the victims, for Socrates was certainly a victim of state violence. On the other, it is a position of innocence, of distancing oneself from any involvement in the violence. For Nietzsche the Platonic dialogue is the "lifeboat" in which all the older poetry and its progeny survived to live on. The scandalized consciousness can, through this new genre, enter "a new world that could never tire of looking at this fantastic spectacle" (69). This is the spectacle of a dying victim (Socrates) for whose death I am not responsible.

Seemingly set over against this, we have Dionysus as the one "of whom marvelous myths relate that he was dismembered by the Titans" (52). At the heart of the myth of Dionysus is also a victim of violence, and Nietzsche is misleading when he says that the "dismemberment, the true Dionysian *suffering*, amounts to a transformation into air, water, earth and fire, and that we should therefore see the condition of individuation as the source and origin of all suffering and hence as something reprehensible" (52). The source and primal ground of all suffering is rather the mob that rips Dionysus from limb to limb. Thus, Nietzsche himself says that the Dionysian phenomenon is a Heraclitean "force that builds the world"—*polemos*, strife or violence (114). At the heart of this myth is violence.

At this point Nietzsche presents his readers with the choice that I outlined above—Socrates or Dionysus. At the same time he shows that they are, in the end, the same thing. The choice of Socrates leads through a 2000-year detour that brings one back to Dionysus. After *The Birth of Tragedy* Nietzsche developed a contrast in which the opposing poles do not collapse into each other and which picks up the strand of Western culture that is treated with silence in *The Birth of Tragedy*: the opposition between Dionysus and the Crucified. For Nietzsche Christianity is part of the problem. It does not help someone to make the difficult choices that a tragic existence entails. Rather, it obscures the choices and makes the noble choices appear base. Thus, he rejects Christianity.

Nietzsche, it seems, would have us look long and hard at the victims of political violence. In this way he seems to be offering an alternative to Plato and the Socratic tradition, but this difference is illusory. In the end the choice for or against Socrates or for or against Dionysus ends in the same violence. They end in the same violence because they have the same origin in scandal: scandal at the violent frenzy of the mob, or scandal at the violent expulsion of this frenzy, or scandal at Nietzsche's bringing them to our attention.

Our journey is to get beyond scandal.

CHAPTER 3

The Scandal of Jean-Jacques Rousseau

Necessary but Impossible Forgiveness

The nature of scandal is such that often, the more one tries to get beyond it, the more deeply ensnared one becomes. We call to mind again Leontius's struggle with looking at the corpses. He wants to look and, at the same time, he is ashamed and angry that he wants to look. The desire provokes the shame and anger, and they, in turn, further inflame the desire. In an analogous way Nietzsche's choice between the rational Socrates and the irrational Dionysus, between the theoretical optimism of the former and the tragic pessimism of the latter, forever leads the reader to expelling either one or the other, thus making the expelled one's return all the more certain. Is there a way beyond this cycle of scandal?

The only way beyond scandal involves going through it, much as the way out of Hell for Dante was to pass through its lowest depths. Given this situation, turning to the texts of Jean-Jacques Rousseau makes sense. Rousseau scandalizes the reader not just with his conceptual positions but also with his self-presentation. Rousseau's self-identification with his texts was essential to his project, which was to occupy the center with everyone else on the periphery. Eric Gans states the case well:

Although many would rather have it otherwise, it seems no exaggeration
to affirm that since the time that Jesus (or one of his disciples) applied to
his individual self the "suffering servant" role of deutero-Isaiah, the most
successful mechanism for self-maintenance in the center of the human universe has been that devised by Jean-Jacques Rousseau. Such mechanisms
are rare, and although their significance comes from the fact that they can
be used by virtually anyone, a particular prestige attaches to their inventors
who acquire, for good or ill, the status of mimetic models.[1]

Over and over again Rousseau's strategy in his texts is to create a position
that implicitly declares: "No one can agree with me." If the reader agrees, she
disagrees with his implicit stance as a writer; and if she should happen to dis-
agree, then indeed she disagrees. This is not just a cheap logical parlor trick,
however. Not only does Rousseau carry out the maneuver with incredible
rhetorical mastery, but he also tries to create a scandalous situation in which
the one thing necessary for the reader is also impossible. I will elaborate on
this strategy below.

Just as scandal cannot be gotten beyond through some better use of our
intellect, so Rousseau's textual strategies cannot be outdone by some more
intricate interpretive moves. Instead, we have to go to the most basic level
of Rousseau's thought and restore what he himself expelled, restore what he
both longs for and fears, restore the one thing that can both complete and
undo his system—forgiveness.

The Scandal of Rousseau's Writings

Rousseau's texts, indeed his whole system of thought, is scandalous in a number of ways, not the least of which is the potent combination of paranoia
concerning others and megalomania concerning himself. It was overtly scandalous in provoking outraged reaction, but it was also scandalous in putting
the reader, as I mentioned at the beginning of this chapter, in a necessarily
impossible position. In order to make the interpretive challenge of Rousseau's texts clear, I focus on the way that scandal informs the entirety of his
writings. The best way to do this is by focusing on what Rousseau himself has
to say about scandal. Rousseau spells out the logic of scandal very clearly, and

this will help us not so much to understand him as point us toward a new way of understanding that can forgive—that is, transform Rousseau's scandalous understanding of scandal into a paradox that reveals the mystery of being.

Rousseau's thinking on scandal was gradually revealed in the scandal that followed the publication of his *Discourse on the Sciences and Arts*. In 1749 the Academy of Dijon announced that it would award thirty *pistoles* of silver for the best essay to answer the question, "Has the restoration of the sciences and the arts tended to purify morals?" Rousseau won the prize with this *Discourse*, which answered "No." His response was heard all over Europe. Since that time and continuing to the present day, the *First Discourse*, as it has come to be called, has produced strong reactions due to its paradoxical nature. Rousseau condemns learning before a learned society.

The *First Discourse* goes beyond clever paradox, however, because it uses the means and institutions of the arts and sciences—a discourse, an academy—to weaken both as well as the academy. Rousseau destroys the very thing that he needs in order to level his criticism. He doesn't just criticize the arts and sciences but he condemns the way they are practiced in contemporary society. Rousseau traces the roots of the arts and sciences to human vice and societal decay. He reveals that what the intelligentsia of eighteenth-century Paris held in such esteem was the cause of the decadence that he was the first to spot.

The *First Discourse* was a broadside launched against all of European culture. In consequence Rousseau became famous, and, as he says, with that "began all my misfortunes."[2] But Rousseau was not a "one-hit" star. In the rest of his writings, and especially in his *Discourse on the Origin and Foundations of Inequality among Men*, he exposed ever more deeply the principles of his line of thought.

Between his *Discourse on the Sciences and Arts* and *Discourse on the Origin and Foundations of Inequality among Men* or *Second Discourse*, Rousseau developed a way of causing scandal without being overtly scandalous. The *First Discourse* was scandalous in the usual or overt fashion. A scandalized Rousseau scandalizes the reader. Rousseau is offended by the corruption that the arts and sciences foment, and he offends educated Europe by pointing out that claim. The *First Discourse*, like Nietzsche's *The Birth of Tragedy*, did not invite silence as a response. Indeed, the *First Discourse* resulted in what has come to be known as the Controversy,[3] which is a series of responses from critics of Rousseau's *First Discourse* and his replies to them. The dispute ended with the publication in 1755 of the *Second Discourse*.

In contrast to both the *First Discourse* and much of the writings in the Controversy, the *Second Discourse* is not a rhetorical attack. In it Rousseau adopts both the tone and methodology of what anachronistically we can call a social scientist. The text prompted Claude Levi-Strauss to call Rousseau the father of modern anthropology.⁴ Using not only his fertile imagination but also the latest in travel reports from the New World, Rousseau imaginatively speculates on the state of nature, which is the opposite of Hobbes' war of all against all. In Rousseau's version humans are isolated, independent, and content—"naturally good." This is perhaps Rousseau's greatest and most lasting contribution to the history of ideas. As he says, "Men are wicked; sad and continual experience spares the need for proof. However, man is naturally good" (*CW* 3:74). With that the myth of the noble savage is born.⁵ We may or may not accept the myth, but we all live in its shadow. Few people are scandalized by it, and those who are, more likely not by but in spite of the way that Rousseau presents it. His rhetoric in the *Second Discourse* is not inflammatory.

Rousseau builds the sense of a necessary impossibility into the very methodology of the *Second Discourse*.⁶ He makes explicit that every step the reader takes toward understanding humankind in the state of nature is, at the same time, a step away from such understanding. Every increase in knowledge, even knowledge of the state of nature, increases our distance from it. The movement toward self-knowledge is, for Rousseau, simultaneously one of self-alienation. To draw close to the state of nature, we must know it (the necessity), but this very knowledge takes us away from it (the impossibility).

The scandal of the *Second Discourse* goes deeper. Rousseau knew, of course, the attempts of Hobbes and Locke to get us to see ourselves in a state of nature, and he judged these attempts failures. According to Rousseau, there is only one way to accomplish this, and that is by "setting aside the facts" of Sacred Scripture.⁷ In other words, one cannot imaginatively get to the state of nature with or through the Bible, yet one cannot get there without it. To know the human sphere, suggests Rousseau, one has to reject the Scriptures. His rejection of the view that we humans are cared for and saved by God's love, however, entails scandal.

This reading turns Rousseau, in effect, on his head. Instead of Rousseau's concept of natural goodness being the basis for his rejection of original sin as a depravity of the human heart, natural goodness itself is the *result* of his rejection of God's salvation and forgiveness. This rejection of forgiveness renders the knowledge of original sin inaccessible. Without a consciousness formed by forgiveness, one is left with a consciousness formed by scandal and thus with natural goodness as a kind of default position. This kind of interpretation is what I mean by a forgiving reading of Rousseau. We can understand his position more deeply by understanding what he is rejecting.

For Christians original sin is not a thing that can be observed. Instead, it is the reality from which they were saved, something that can be understood only in light of salvation.[8] I say "reality from which they were saved," but that is somewhat misleading. Original sin, like all evil, has no reality in itself. It is parasitic on the good, a distortion of true love and desire. Thus, it can only be seen for what it is by being seen for what it is *not*, by being seen in light of the reality which it mimics. Rousseau rejects this light and thereby loses the ability to see.

Rousseau's system cannot be interpreted correctly as the straightforward development of his principle of natural goodness, though some have tried.[9] Since his reaction against proffered forgiveness is the abiding source of the principle of natural goodness, Rousseau's system finds its ultimate ground not in this principle but the reaction that leads to it. As I said earlier, the term for this reaction to forgiveness offered by a crucified savior is "scandal." Hence, my thesis is that *Rousseau's system is rooted in scandal.* There are two ways of reading him, one that gets caught up in the scandal and the other that forgives it. The scandal of Rousseau derives from his scandal at Christ, which leads to his spreading scandal to others. These two senses of the term *scandal*—refusing forgiveness and leading others into sin—are two sides of the same coin. They are tantamount to inhabiting a universe in which there is no forgiveness.

A Hermeneutics of Forgiveness

It may come as a surprise that Rousseau began his life as a writer by prophesying about his need for forgiveness. In the preface to the *Discourse on the Sciences and Arts*, he writes: "I foresee that I will not easily be forgiven for the side I have dared to take" (*CW* 2:3).[10] Rousseau understood that his position or "side" both required forgiveness and made it difficult. In his later years he declared that any needed forgiveness had become impossible, but not through any fault of his own. He maintained that he would never be forgiven by others for the evil that *they* had done *against him*. In his very fine article "Ils ne me pardonneront jamais le mal qu'ils m'ont fait" ("'They Will Never Pardon Me for the Evil They Have Done Me'"), Frédéric S. Eigeldinger gives considerable textual evidence to show that the notion of never receiving forgiveness for the wrongs that others had done him is a theme running through much of Rousseau's writings and correspondence.[11] In 1768 Rousseau hung an inscription in his room titled "The Attitudes of the Various Sections of the Public Towards Me." Twice, in reference to Swiss magistrates, he remarks that they "hate me because of the wrong they have done me."[12] A similar expression occurs in his *Letter to Beaumont* (1763): "I have been surrounded by spies and by the malicious; and the world is full of people who hate me because of the harm they have done me" (*CW* 9:49).[13] Further, this idea of his not being forgiven is connected with Rousseau's thoughts on scandal. He thus writes to Mylord Maréchal that the ministers of the Gospel, "after having established in principle their competence over all scandals, excite scandal toward such objects as they please and then[,] in virtue of the scandal they have caused, take the affair to the judge. . . . The foolish ministers [of Neuchatel] hate me all more because of the harm they cannot do me."[14] Rousseau lived in a state of constant scandal.

Rousseau's stance as a writer grew progressively more estranged from his readers. This is especially true of his autobiographical writings. The *Confessions* is the last book he wrote addressed to his contemporaries. *Rousseau Judge of Jean-Jacques: Dialogues* is addressed to future generations. As for his final work, *The Reveries of the Solitary Walker*, Rousseau writes: "My enterprise is the same as Montaigne's, but my goal is the complete opposite of his: he wrote his *Essays* only for others, and I write my reveries only for myself" (*CW* 8:8).

We are reading his texts in a way that allows them to speak to us as readers, even if that goes against Rousseau's stated intention. There are, of course, many places in his corpus in which Rousseau, with his frequent use of direct address, invites our participation in his work. But our particular form of participation is not determined by Rousseau's invitation or lack thereof. Instead, in the words of Nicholas Boyle's discussion of secular texts in general, we seek to speak "a word that opens the way back to the origin of those [secular] writings in God—in the primal and unfulfillable commandment to responsibility and in the primal act of forgiveness by which God has taken on himself all the pain of our failure to fulfill it."[15] For Boyle the task is both to uncover the limit that constitutes the writing as secular and to bring to it the knowledge of what lies beyond, so that the limit is recognized as such. Boyle states that the word one brings to the text must "read the point of trespass, the point which makes the writing secular, the point at which God is forgotten, as the point of forgiveness, the point at which God is incarnate, both revealed and hidden in flesh."[16] By bringing a word of forgiveness to the text, the reader can say: "These words . . . say what it is about us that needs to be redeemed."[17]

Boyle suggests, rightly in my view, that there is a divide between secular and sacred writings that can be acknowledged, respected, and in some sense bridged by the reader who brings those secular writings back to their "origin . . . in God." I want to amplify this suggestion in that I think some writings, like Rousseau's, violently contest both this divide and the attempt at a restoration to their origin. This is not because Rousseau was somehow more resolutely atheistic than, say, his materialistic counterparts in eighteenth-century Paris. They walked away from God and didn't look back. Rousseau, however, was unable to do that. He was too much in rivalry with the Scriptures, with Christ, with God himself simply to walk away. Instead he engages again and again in an attempt to overcome Christianity. We find in his writings the double movement of approach and avoidance, acceptance and rejection, embrace and pushing away, a longing to look on God and the severe determination to have God look at him. We find, in a word, scandal.

Our reading of Rousseau is an attempt to overcome the scandal by restoring to his system that which the system has not only rejected but around whose rejection it has structured itself: forgiveness. This will undo his system. Rousseau says more clearly than anyone else "what it is about us that needs to be redeemed." Therein lies his great value. What stands in the center of his system is scandal—that is, rejection of Christ crucified. What has been expelled gives shape and order to what remains, and the remaining system allows one to see the shape of what is missing. In Boyle's words, "Even in the works and words that seem to hide God's face, or to spit on it, we can see God revealed at the heart of our world and in our culture."[18]

As we begin to read Rousseau, we face a profound paradox that encompasses the impossible necessity of scandal. The fact is that we do not know what is to be forgiven in his text; that which needs to be forgiven will only reveal itself if, in some sense, it has already been forgiven. One cannot just perform, however, some act of general absolution over a text and expect it to be understood. Each text has to be read in terms of its own texture and history so that the particular form of forgiving understanding emerges from the encounter with the particular text itself. We are to read with great care, lifting up gently those things that need to be redeemed but doing so in the certainty that they are already, indeed, redeemed.[19] Only as *forgiven* sin will sin reveal itself *as sin*. Only in bringing what lies beyond the text to the text will the text tell us "what it is about us that needs to be redeemed."

The *topos* of scandal can help the reader to enter into this process. By identifying that which is scandalous, the reader reaches a deeper understanding of the blocks to, as well as the opportunities for, forgiveness. Earlier we defined scandal as promised access being blocked. In order to understand not just scandal but also forgiveness in a way that will be more useful for interpretation, I want to expand on this definition. A text causes scandal when it demands of the interpreter something that is simultaneously necessary and impossible—that is, when it puts the reader in a position in which she wants to understand yet cannot. She cannot move forward in the quest for understanding but still must. The reason why this situation is scandalous and not paradoxical is that a paradox is a seeming contradiction that leads to ever deepening thought, understanding, and love. Scandals, on the other hand, are blocks to thought, understanding, and love. Interpretation is the art of transforming scandals into paradoxes. In a very real sense the art of forgiving interpretation tries to meet the impossible necessity or necessary impossibility of scandal by allowing new possibilities to emerge and unbinding the text from necessity. It does this by restoring that which has been rejected, thus both completing and undoing the text. It now has to be shown how this works in practice with the texts of Rousseau.

Rousseau's Thoughts on Scandal

Some of Rousseau's direct statements on scandal illuminate how he conceived of it. Rousseau was forced to deal with scandal because during the Controversy his adversaries accused him of causing it.

Some of the severest warnings in the New Testament were reserved for those who caused scandal. These teachings were developed by the Christian community as cautions against causing others to sin by one's bad example or by making public anything that would weaken social institutions, especially the Church. Rousseau offended people in his *Discourse on the Sciences and Arts*. He was accused of leading others into sin by his praise of ignorance and his criticism of learning. Knowing that his praise of ignorance and scorn for the arts and sciences was scandalous, Rousseau both confirms and upends the Christian understanding of scandal by writing that there are two kinds of ignorance, a "ferocious and brutal ignorance" as well as "another reasonable kind of ignorance . . . [that] is born from a lively love of virtue." "That is the ignorance I praised," he adds, "and one I request from Heaven as punishment for the scandal I caused the scholarly by my stated scorn for human Sciences" (*CW* 2:51–52).

However, the most acerbic criticism of Rousseau was directed against his critique of manners. Rousseau saw cultivated behavior, manners, as being simply a form of hypocrisy overlaid on interior corruption. He consequently advocated directness in communication. As for those in his own society, he remarked, if one only listened to their language, one would think that they were of the highest morals, but if one actually looked at what they did, one would see that they were more depraved than the "savages" about whom missionaries and explorers wrote. In his *Letter to Mr. Grimm* Rousseau writes that what M. Gautier notices he himself acknowledges: "The people could not speak a more decent language than that of our century."[20] However, Rousseau sees further that these same people "could not have more corrupt morals." He adds, "and that is what scandalizes me" (*CW* 2:87).

The counterattacks against Rousseau were scandalized reactions to this scandalous assault on society. They can be summarized as follows: You would take away that which distinguishes us from the animals and thereby makes us not more virtuous but more plainly vicious.

Specifically, in his *Reply to the Discourse* Stanislaus Leszinski, King of Poland, posed the most direct question to Rousseau concerning scandal.[21] The King asked whether Rousseau would have the veneer of society simply discarded since it often serves as a mask for hypocrisy: "Would he wish then for vice to appear openly, for indecency to be joined to disorder and scandal to crime?" (*CW* 2:34). Rousseau is quite certain that he would prefer to have vice appear openly rather than hide and attack him from behind. He, and society as a whole, would be safer as a result. But as to whether scandal should be joined to crime, Rousseau's answer is "I do not know" (*CW* 2:49). This response is more significant than it might at first appear. Of all the objections raised by various critics during the five years of the Controversy, this is the only one to which Rousseau admits that he does not have an answer. In contrast, he elsewhere explains why he is able to answer his critics:

> I meditated on my subject at length and deeply, and I tried to consider all aspects of it. I doubt that any of my adversaries can say as much. At least I don't perceive in their writings any of those luminous truths that are no less striking in their obviousness than in their novelty, and that are always the fruit and proof of an adequate meditation. I dare say that they have never raised a reasonable objection that I did not anticipate and to which I did not reply in advance. That is why I am always compelled to restate the same things. (*CW* 2:110fn)

What Rousseau does gives us in replying to Leszinski's specific objection, in a very lapidary form, is his position concerning scandal:

> I prefer to have my enemy attack me with open force than to come up treacherously and strike me from behind. What then! Must scandal be combined with crime? I do not know, but I surely wish that deceit were not combined with it. All the maxims about scandal to which we have been treated for so long are very convenient for the vicious: if one wished to follow them rigorously, one must allow himself to be robbed, betrayed, and killed with impunity, and never punish anyone; for a scoundrel on the rack is a very scandalous thing. (*CW* 2:49)

Rousseau's rhetoric nudges the reader toward thinking that his admission of ignorance as regards this particular objection is purely rhetorical. After that bare admission Rousseau appears to argue that scandal ought, in fact, to be joined to crime. I want to argue, however, that Rousseau is not simply asserting a personal lack of knowledge or understanding that could be remedied with either more information or deeper reflection. Instead, he is raising the possibility of a more radical limit to reason itself. The question raised by the King is beyond the competence of reason as Rousseau knows it.

I will grant that there are several levels on which one can read Rousseau's "I do not know." On a pragmatic level it could be that Rousseau is afraid of the authorities. If Rousseau were to answer, as it seems his position would warrant, "Yes, scandal is to be joined to crime," he would be contradicting the teaching of the Church, both Protestant and Catholic, leaving him open to charges of causing social unrest. This is something that Rousseau does not want to happen. Here is what he wrote in the unpublished *Preface to a Second Letter to Bordes* (cf. *CW* 2:5): "If the Discourse of Dijon alone excited so many murmurs and caused so much scandal, what would have happened if I had from the first instant developed the entire extent of a System that is true but distressing, of which the question treated in this Discourse is only a Corollary? A declared enemy of the violence of the wicked, I would at the very least have passed for the enemy of public tranquility" (*CW* 2:184). I still think it is incumbent on the interpreter, however, to look for reasons internal to Rousseau's logic rather than accepting that scandal is to be forbidden or allowed due to some external force like the ecclesiastical authorities. This means finding something in Rousseau's argument that would make him shy away from affirming his right to "join scandal to crime."

On a first reading Rousseau's argument can be reconstructed in the following way. He assumes the position of his opponent that scandal cannot be joined to crime and that the maxims concerning scandal are to be rigorously obeyed. If this were so, then one could not punish criminals because that would be joining scandal (public punishment) to crime. The reason for this is that public punishment is a very scandalous thing. But if punishing criminals is not possible, then the virtuous citizens of a society are going to be routinely robbed and killed. This is an unacceptable conclusion stemming from his opponents' premise that scandal is not allowed. As Rousseau states, their position is "very convenient for the vicious." Rousseau's conclusion, although he never states it, would be that under certain circumstances scandal is indeed necessary. He has, in effect, turned the King's argument against him by showing that, although the King is accusing Rousseau of advocating a position that would increase public disorder, it is the King's own position that leads to disorder.

Of course, there is clearly another level to the argument. Rousseau says that, if the maxims about scandal were followed rigorously, "one must allow himself to be robbed, betrayed, and killed with impunity." Even if we grant that not torturing criminals would leave us exposed to a lawless society, the presence of the word "betrayed" in Rousseau's argument should give us pause. Criminals are not usually accused of betraying the people whom they rob or kill. Rousseau includes this word to indicate to the careful reader that he is thinking of a particular case of following the maxims about scandal—the case of Jesus Christ. Here we see the first indication of his real uncertainty. Is allowing oneself to be "robbed, betrayed, and killed with impunity" an outcome to be avoided? If it is, Rousseau's argument leads to the conclusion that scandal can sometimes be allowed. But most of his critics were avowed Christians. Would they accept this premise? I do not know, and neither did Rousseau. Thus his uncertainty.

Both levels of this argument hinge on the premise that "the scoundrel on the rack is a very scandalous thing." What does Rousseau mean by this? It is difficult to imagine he means that the scoundrel on the rack is a sight that would induce weaker members of the community to sin or fall. One of the purposes of putting thieves on the rack was to discourage others from this form of sinning. The punishment would have been judged an "edifying" sight, capable of building up the proper order, the exact opposite of scandal.

Rousseau goes further, however, by intuiting that the "scoundrel on the rack" is a scandalous sight because of Christ on the cross. The French word used here for "rack" is *roue*.[22] It refers to a circular rack upon which the prisoner lay. If one looks at engravings from the time, it is clear the prisoner was placed upon this rack with arms and legs outstretched to form a cross. The criminal on the rack thus resembles Christ on the Cross. Hence the scandal of the scene.

Rousseau, a careful reader of Plato, has moved beyond Plato here. For Plato the executioner's corpses that Leontius comes upon were also a scandalous sight, but he could not resolve this scandal except to split the soul and hope to find enough available "spiritedness" or anger to overcome the desire to look. The ideal for Plato would be not to look, since reason cannot grasp what it is seeing.[23]

Rousseau, however, "sees" that what is revealed in the Cross is the identity of Christ crucified with the scoundrel on the rack. He cannot accept this identification because truly understanding that Christ is the scoundrel on the rack is to accept the forgiveness of the victim and to annul the scandal. For his argument to work Rousseau needs the scandal of the Cross to make the scoundrel on the rack a very scandalous thing, but he cannot accept the consequences of his own premise. Hence, Rousseau would also like to hold the position that scandal is not allowed. Scandal gets his argument going but carries it too far. It reveals the dependence of his thought on Christ.

The victim of society's violence offers access to a mystery and yet blocks it. We seem to catch a glimpse in the victim of something deeper, but our vision is also blocked by the victim. The veil cannot be lifted so long as the scoundrel on the rack remains only a scandalous thing. Christ is a scandal and remains a scandal for as long as people look upon him as one accursed by God, which is what his death certainly seemed to indicate to his fellow Jews. Faith in the Resurrection changes the vision into a recognition of God's power. By this, the shameful death on the Cross is not abrogated or written off as a mistake now that Christ's disciples believe he is the Son of God. Rather, the Crucifixion becomes necessary and fulfills the Scriptures.

Rousseau wants us to look at the scoundrel on the rack and understand something about society. This is the way his argument works against his opponents. But he is also aware on some level that we can only sustain that gaze and reach that depth of vision by realizing that Christ himself was once that scoundrel on the rack and so identified himself with the outcast, the criminal, and the marginalized. It is only when the scoundrel ceases to be regarded as a scoundrel and becomes a human being that the sight of him stretched out on the rack becomes capable of producing knowledge. In this way Christ himself creates the possibility of a kind of scandal that reveals the limitations of our law and social order. It also reveals the limitations of our reason. The desire to look can still be scandalous, internally conflicted, but it leads somewhere else. One can get beyond the scandal through forgiveness—not by forgiving the scandal but by receiving forgiveness from this "scoundrel" for what we have done to him.

If I am correct in seeing Christ as present in Rousseau's system as the one who renders the victim scandalous, then that is also the limit of his presence. Christ is always and only for Rousseau a scandal, a figure of expulsion who continues to fascinate in being expelled. The presence of Christ as the scandalous scoundrel on the rack corresponds to the absence of Christ as a forgiving presence. That is, for Rousseau to be able to see the scoundrel on the rack as a very scandalous thing puts *Rousseau* in a scandalous position. Does he let the criminal go and thus let society degenerate, or does he create another victim? These are his only two choices, and thus Rousseau truly does not know, cannot see or understand whether "scandal is to be joined to crime." Rousseau works to avoid letting this question be put to him directly. Instead, he develops his system so that he is the one on the rack. There is no forgiveness, only scandal.

The Path Traversed Thus Far

We have seen that scandal is an anthropological phenomenon rooted in the way that language structures our consciousness. It is not enough to say that language reveals as well as conceals; one has to say that it is precisely insofar as language reveals that it conceals. One cannot write with the word *pencil*, but the more that the word *pencil* is unlike the physical object of the actual writing instrument, the better it can represent it.

Nietzsche showed us how the philosophical attempt, represented in the figure of Socrates, to deal with scandal ends in its only alternative, the Dionysian frenzy of sacrificial violence. Rousseau shows in an even more radical way that scandal is beyond the grasp of reason, that all scandal ultimately is a "scandal of reason." He is led inexorably to the necessary yet impossible choice of either a disordered society creating victims or creating victims to have an ordered society.

The dilemma that Rousseau faces becomes our dilemma in facing Rousseau. Do we condemn him or join him in condemning others? There does not seem to be any third option. We have reached an impasse in our journey through scandal with Rousseau. How, then, are we to proceed?

We need to find a way of dealing with scandal. For this to happen, however, it is necessary to read Rousseau—that is, to read the story of humanity without God (*Discourse on the Sciences and Arts, Discourse on the Origin and Foundations of Inequality among Men, Emile*), and of Rousseau isolated more and more from everyone (autobiographical writings), and still find "the retrospective illumination by faith from the standpoint of the ending, a conversion."[24] Without this perspective the words of Rousseau pose the danger of turning hearts to stone. The constant danger of getting stuck on the surface, in the literal meaning of Rousseau's text, and of never penetrating to the deeper meaning is real. The reader constantly encounters obstacles to understanding, as is evidenced by the many books that accuse Rousseau of inconsistency bordering on incomprehensibility. Is there a hermeneutics that could transform the scandalous veil of Rousseau's writing into a revelation that would allow continuation of the journey? As Christ sheds light backward on the Old Testament, can he shed light forward on Rousseau?

For Rousseau the geography of scandal is such that it creates a world without forgiveness, and that can serve as a passable definition of Hell. How are we to traverse Hell? To do this I turn first to Dante and then to Scripture.

Dante and Rousseau as authors are not as far apart as may appear. Both can still scandalize readers. All of Dante's greatness as a poet, as William Franke remarks, has not eliminated "a certain taste of scandal attaching to so audaciously self-centered and self-willed an outlook on such a megalomaniac scale."[25] For his part Rousseau wrote that at the Last Judgment he would approach the Almighty with a copy of his *Confessions* in hand as a form of undeniable self-justification. He considered his novel *Emile* a book that would change the world for the better, if only people would understand it and put it into practice.

Furthermore, both authors involve themselves in the text in such a way that it can be difficult to differentiate between text and author. The interpenetration of author and character in their writing makes it difficult to distinguish fact from fiction, autobiography from story. Franke remarks:

> Dante's poem programmatically places this ineluctable structural condition [the complementary indebtedness of every poetic production to some historically existing individual and that individual to some historically conditioned poetic fiction] center-stage of the fiction itself, blurring the boundary between fact and fiction in reaching toward their common origin in interpretation, in this instance in the mutual belonging of Dante as literary invention and as historical personage together, since the one would not be what it is at all without the other. (3–4)

Rousseau uses this same structural condition, especially in his autobiographical writings, for very different ends from Dante. Rousseau is Jean-Jacques, the tutor in *Emile*. He is the main character of his autobiographical writings. He even splits himself into two characters, Rousseau and Jean-Jacques, in *Rousseau Judge of Jean-Jacques: Dialogues*.[26] Rousseau, like Dante, deliberately blurs the boundary between the historical figure and the literary creation in order to reveal just how much of each is constituted by interpretation. Rousseau's own reading of his life is his attempt to teach us how to read such texts.

It would be an oversimplification but not inaccurate to say that, while Dante is trying to direct the reader's eyes to the transcendent mystery that is the summation of all loves, Rousseau is trying to direct the gaze to himself. Still, both Dante and Rousseau want to force the reader to *interpret* and to be aware of their interpretation. The realities that each presents, especially of themselves, never pretend to be unmediated, detached views given in some value-free space. The reader only gets to the figure of Dante or Jean-Jacques through an act of interpretation, figuring either the one or the other as a certain kind of person.

Rousseau was the first literary celebrity. His writings, as well as others' writings about him, made him both loved and hated, feted and condemned. When *Emile* earned him condemnation and banishment instead of praise and reward, he continued to write as one accused, constantly defending both his thought and his person.[27] Dante also suffered banishment and wrote the *Divine Comedy* in exile. Certainly there is a strong element of self-justification in that work. However, neither Rousseau nor Dante is a great writer because of his attempts at self-justification. Rather, their greatness lies in their ability to invite, cajole, and even force the reader to become more self-aware in her interpretation of their respective texts.

Both Dante and Rousseau write of Hell. Dante gives us a vivid description of a physical place that allows one to grasp its spiritual dimensions, while Rousseau details the psychology of being abandoned in a dark abyss. Trips through Hell are not, Dante makes clear, without their dangers. Dante, the author as well as the character, overcomes the obstacles and, in so doing, teaches the reader how to overcome them. We need to look carefully at how this is accomplished.

CHAPTER 4

The Interpretation of Dante Alighieri

Closing One's Eyes in Order to See

In Canto IX of the *Inferno* the character Dante is standing outside the city of Dis. Dante's descent has reached an impasse at the gates of this city. The devils who guard the city refuse to listen to Virgil's entreaties. The Furies then appear and threaten the appearance of the Medusa. Virgil has to cover Dante's eyes with his own hands to make sure that he does not look upon the Gorgon and turn to stone. One look would be enough to ensure that Dante could not continue the journey. The feelings evoked by this scene are those of frustration, fear, and danger because of being threatened with blindness. Looking at the Medusa directly will turn one into stone, but not overcoming the present obstacle will also end the journey. What is the pilgrim to do?

Dante as author chooses this moment to address the reader directly.[1]

O you who have sound intellects,
look at the doctrine which hides itself
beneath the veil of these strange verses.
(IX, 61–63)[2]

At the very moment in the poem that the character Dante's vision is being blocked by Virgil's careful hands, the author commands the reader to look more deeply and to interpret. More specifically, Dante tells us that the *versi strani*, strange verses, are a veil beneath which hides a *dottrina* or doctrine. So we have somehow to remove or get beneath the veil of strange verses. This task is, perhaps, analogous to Mark Danner's call that we get beneath the surface of society and find out what is really going on. For Dante this involves looking away from the spectacle that holds us captive. William Franke tells us that "the reader['s] . . . immediate vision, or literal reading, encounters a veil that hides a deeper truth. Indeed, the reader, no less than the protagonist, has been scandalized, that is, absorbed in the spectacle of Hell as Dante has vividly depicted it up to this point, but is then called upon to see through to the doctrine veiled beneath the myth."[3] Dante, in other words, is encouraging the reader to close his or her eyes to the surface meaning, while opening them to a veiled meaning. In effect, one has to look away and approach the text indirectly, through certain hermeneutical procedures.

What leads a reader to the kind of interpretation that tries to get "beneath the veil" of a text are the obstacles to understanding that it presents. Dante is proposing that one *not* just look at his poem more closely but rather that one turn away in order to understand it. If one were to look directly at the Medusa, one would turn to stone and be unable to continue the journey. Certain sights petrify the understanding, inducing a kind of intellectual trauma to which the cry of Leontius may well be pointing. Dante scholar John Freccero suggests that this "petrification is an interpretive as well as moral threat and that the act of interpretation depends on a moral condition."[4] Petrification, he suggests, is the "inability to see the light of truth in an interpretive glance."[5] The passage from Dante is meant to help us overcome this danger.

Nonetheless, according to Freccero, the words of this direct address have "always represented something of a scandal in the interpretation of Dante's allegory, primarily because they seem to fail their didactic intent: the *dottrina* referred to here remains as veiled to us as it was to the poet's contemporaries."[6] I need to draw attention here to the way in which the very effort by Dante to help the reader overcome her scandal, her obstacle to understanding, has historically generated not deeper understanding but more scandal. My critical point is very near the surface. The attempt to overcome a scandalized consciousness can fail and lead to more scandal. The risks that Dante runs in the construction of *The Divine Comedy* are not all fictional.

Freccero overcomes the scandal of the passage by seeing it as a clue to overcoming scandal in reading, and he does this by specifying to what the words "strange verses" refer. That is, he closes his eyes to the text in front of him and finds another referent outside the first text. Having ascertained that, he is able also to specify the doctrine. Paradoxically he ends up looking more closely at the text as a result of having looked away. Freccero sees this address to the reader as pointing to an exemplary occasion of Dante's practice of Christian allegory, which, he argues, is "identical with the phenomenology of confession, for both involve a comprehension of the self in history within a retrospective literary structure."[7] In this canto, as he would have it, Dante is implicitly confessing a sin forgiven to point to the deeper reality revealed by the forgiveness.

A phenomenology of confession implies the context of sin forgiven. One does not confess one's sins simply in order to have them forgiven, however, but in the faith that they are already forgiven. The confession, like allegory, allows one to overcome the blockage that scandal entails and to move more deeply into the reality of forgiving love. In other words, forgiveness does not simply remove sin; it also opens up new possibilities of meaning.

At this juncture we can profitably compare Rousseau and Dante on the point of confession. The whole of the preface to the *Discourse on Inequality* is structured according to what is "easy to see" and what is "more difficult to see." Rousseau analyzes the question about the origin of inequality so that he leads the reader beyond what is clearly visible to what is harder to see. That is, Rousseau, like Dante, also practices a phenomenology of confession, and not just in the *Confessions*. He is always trying to comprehend the self in history within a retrospective literary structure.[8] He, like Dante, also uses direct address at critical moments: "O Man, whatever country you may be from, whatever your opinions may be, listen: here is your history as I believed it to read, not in the Books of your Fellow-man, who are liars, but in Nature, which never lies" (*CW* 3:19). The differences between Dante's project and Rousseau's are also clear. Dante is urging the reader to get beyond his words, his strange verses, to a true teaching. He is implicitly invoking the Bible with a number of allusions ("sound intellect," "doctrine," "veil," "verses") and, most of all, making this address precisely at the moment when the character Dante is allowing Virgil to shield his eyes, demonstrating a real trust in tradition and reason, a real trust in his "Fellow-man." None of this is true for Rousseau. Scripture is set aside, and Rousseau will now read to us from the book of Nature. One's "Fellow-man" is a liar.

The reason for these differences is the respective authors' relationship to scandal. Dante is trying to teach a way through scandal; Rousseau is trying to entrap the reader in it. Everyone for Rousseau is to end up scandalized, but in such a way that the only thing anyone can see is the difference between oneself and another.

Another way to grasp the difference between Dante and Rousseau is to recognize both the similarities and differences in the way they use Scripture. Dante's way is rooted in the New Testament practice of reading the Old Testament with the veil lifted in such a way that the Old Testament discloses Christ but "set[s] aside" the Old Testament (2 Cor. 3:14). This "setting aside" paradoxically implies a constant return to the Old Testament to see ever more deeply the way in which it points to Christ, the ways in which he fulfills it and thus sets it aside. Rousseau, for his part, famously begins the *Discourse on Inequality* by "setting aside all the facts," those being primarily of Creation as recounted in Genesis (*CW* 3:19).[9] In this way the New Testament, Dante, and Rousseau all share a setting aside of the Old Testament, but the similarity is all on the surface. The way in which the first two do it is diametrically opposed to Rousseau's, who denies the Scriptures the chance of revealing anything. His setting aside serves to open up the theoretical space of the state of nature. Scripture is then left behind.

Here I wish to follow Dante and look more closely at the way he sees this "setting aside." The figure of the veil that hides the doctrine in Dante's direct address is an allusion to the Pauline tradition of biblical hermeneutics. In the Second Letter to the Corinthians, Paul speaks of the veil that covered Moses' face as the figurative relationship between the two Testaments. Paul contrasts the Old and New Testaments, the former's letters veiled, while the latter's spirit is Christ who reveals. Freccero summarizes:

> The significance of the letter is in its final term, Christ, who was present all along, but revealed as the spirit only at the end, the conversion of the Old Testament to the New. Understanding the truth is not then a question of critical intelligence applied here and there, but rather of a retrospective illumination by faith from the standpoint of the ending, a conversion.[10]

For Dante the Christ event was the end term that gives us a chance to read history according to a meaning. "The 'then' and 'now' of the Old and the New Testament were at once the continuity and discontinuity of universal history, the letter and the spirit respectively of God's revelation."[11] For Rousseau, as I have tried to show, Christ is also the final term but only the rejected end or missing part of the whole system. Christ provides a meaning to the whole only in a negative way—the one necessary to the system who cannot possibly be included in it.

For all the differences between Dante and Rousseau, there is still no reason why the hermeneutic procedure implicit in Dante's poem cannot be extended to Rousseau's text. If Dante is consciously trying to get us to lift the veil and discover the words of eternal life, we still can read Rousseau, against his own design, as doing the same thing. Thus, the possibility of reading Rousseau as revealing Christ was bequeathed to the West by Dante. His poem took all the knowledge of the medieval world and *interpreted* it in such a way that he showed how it both flowed out of and back into the "love that moves the Sun and the other stars." This way of interpreting is not always at hand. In fact, I want to argue that it can emerge only as a kind of subversion of the normal way of interpreting a text.

The passage in which Dante, the character, is threatened with the arrival of Medusa, can be interpreted as Dante, the author, commenting on scandal and interpretation. Scandal comes in a variety of forms. The danger of the Medusa, the reason she can turn the hearts of men (traditionally she has no effect on women) to stone, is her erotic beauty.[12] So the Medusa is not the defiled corpses by which Leontius is tempted. Still, violence is obviously an element in this story. The Furies scream out for her to come, and when they do, they recall the assault of Theseus: "Poorly did we avenge the assault of Theseus" (IX, 54). The goal of Theseus's descent into the underworld was an erotic assault on Persephone.

Freccero sees in the Medusa episode a representation by Dante of the temporality of his own introspection, of an actual danger narrowly avoided, of a scandal overcome, of a former illusion seen by Dante for what it is. For Freccero the figure of the Medusa is apt for representing the kind of retrospective judgment that characterizes both confession and allegory. There are real dangers in this retrospective glance, the traditional one being nostalgia. What gives this passage its temporal dimension is that the "strange verses" of Canto IX echo lines from an earlier poem of Dante's *Rime Petrose*. I can do no better than follow Freccero in his discovery, who quotes a passage from one of the *Rime Petrose* (43c, 53–60). These lines "paint a wintry scene described by a despairing lover."[13] Here is the Italian original:

> Versan le vene le fummifere acque
> per li vapor che la terra ha nel ventre,
> che d'abisso li tira suso in *alto;*
> onde cammino al bel giorno mi piacque
> che ora è fatto rivo, e sarà mentre
> che durerà del verno il grande *assalto;*
> la terra fa un suol che par di *smalto,*
> e l'acqua morta si converte in vetro.

[The springs spew forth fumy waters / because the earth draws the gases / that are in its bowels upwards from the abyss; / a path that pleased me in fine weather / is now a stream, and so will remain / as long as winter's great onslaught endures; / the earth has formed a crust like rock / and dead waters turn into glass.]

The rhyme scheme of this passage is mirrored in that of the Medusa passage in *The Divine Comedy*:

> Con l'unghie si fendea ciascuna il petto;
> battiensi a palme e gridavan si *alto,*
> ch'i' mi strinsi al poeta per sospetto.
> "Vegna Medusa: sì 'l farem di *smalto,"*
> dicevan tutte riguardando in giuso;
> "mal non vengiammo in Tesëo l'*assalto."*
> (IX, 49–54)

[Each was tearing her breast with her nails; / and they were beating themselves with their hands, / and crying out so loudly that in fear I pressed close to the poet. / "Let Medusa come and we'll turn him to stone," / they all cried, looking downward. / "Poorly did we avenge the assault of Theseus."]

Freccero explains the parallel in the following way:

> The description of a world without love, matching the poet's winter of
> the soul, contains exactly the rhyme words from Dante's description of
> the Medusa, sibilants that might qualify as *versi strani* in the address to
> the reader. Thus a passage that threatens petrification recalls, in a reified,
> concrete way, precisely the poem that described such a reification at the
> hands of a kind of Medusa. The words themselves reflect each other in
> such a way that they constitute a short-circuit across the temporal distance
> that separates the two moments of poetic history, a block that threatens to
> make further progress impossible. For the reader, the parallel threat is to
> refuse to see the allegory through the letter, to ignore the double focus of
> the *versi strani*. The echo of the *Rime Petrose* is an invitation to the reader
> to measure the distance that separates the *now* of the poet from the *then*
> of his *persona;* in the fiction of the poem, the Medusa is, like the lady of
> stone, no historic character at all, but the poet's own creation. Its threat is
> the threat of idolatry.[14]

The strange verses tell of an imaginary figure that can turn the person who
looks upon her into stone. The doctrine to which they refer is the way an
unrestrained love of a creature can turn the heart to stone, making it incapable of life and knowing. But these same verses and this same doctrine have
another dimension. The poem also tells us that even when the way forward
seems blocked progress is possible by having one's eyes closed and waiting for
the celestial messenger. The experience taught Dante, and now he teaches
his reader that each can be delivered from the letter that causes death and
understand it in a way that advances life.

The poet Dante asks the reader to bring a certain kind of understanding into existence. The hidden doctrine can only be seen by those of "sound
intellect." For the moment we can assume that humanity's default position
is one of an unsound intellect. This contributes to the hidden nature of the
doctrine. Franke aptly summarizes for us Freccero's position in this matter:
the Medusa "lines up . . . with the letter that kills while the Pauline image of
lifting the veil, or 'revelation,' figures a hermeneutic procedure whereby the
spirit gives life."[15] We have, then, two seemingly opposed possibilities: the

text either can be the cause of words that figuratively get written on stone—
that is, petrify the heart—or the same text, the same words, can be read as
life-giving. In fact, we could say that Dante's text is both the Medusa and
the possibility of life. The text, with all its beauty and power to fascinate, can
captivate the reader and turn his heart to stone, or the reader can turn away
from it in order to await the celestial messenger who will "open" the text.

In the poem the Medusa does not appear. What appears to Dante *now*
is the fascination of a dark eros that is seen by his understanding, due to his
conversion, as ugly and repulsive. Dante does not allow any nostalgia for his
former sin. A messenger from heaven then comes, rebukes the devils, and
commands the door to open so that Virgil and Dante can continue.

This episode suggests that there are certain kinds of experiences, certain
kinds of understanding, that can petrify one's heart and mind. Such is the
risk of traversing Hell. The power to prevent or evade such experiences is
not innate or attributable to the application of "critical intelligence." Rather,
if the door opens, it is owing to something for which we cannot take credit.
That the opening of the door to the City of Dis was directed by God is clear
only to Dante the poet from the perspective of the ending which is a conversion. The Medusa cannot appear because, had she done so, there would be
no poet or poem. Rather, idolatry would have followed, and the one whose
heart is turned to stone writes petrified verses, not the *Divine Comedy*.[16] The
Medusa is a figure of scandal—an obstruction that prevents one from going
forward. The only writing that results from it is the letter that kills. For the
true doctrine hidden beneath the veil to be revealed, for the scandal to be
overcome, more is needed.

In Rousseau, by his own intention, there is no true allegory of seeing
through the letter. The letter, instead, points solely to Rousseau. The only
transcendent meaning is the false transcendence of the heroic martyr, Jean-
Jacques. Rousseau's texts are not meant to open up to any other transcendence. They are designed to trap the reader in a scandalous relationship with
the author. Rousseau's texts, like Dante's, have obstructions that threaten to
make further progress impossible. The difference is that Rousseau intends
this block to remain just that—a block. Dante, on the other hand, hopes
that the reader will transform the block to a bridge, and he indicates as much
within the poem itself. For his part Rousseau cannot prevent the reader from
transforming that block into a bridge; he cannot prevent the reader from

seeing the allegory through the letter. The double focus exists, even though he rejects it. Thus Rousseau's writings, in spite of themselves, reveal the rejected Christ.

Freccero's analysis helps us to link these insights with those of the first chapter because he ties the threat of idolatry represented by Dante's creation of the Medusa to both desire and to language. There is, he observes, "the reaching out in desire for what mortals can never possess and the reaching out of language for the significance of silence."[17] We as readers have to see that both desire (especially the desire to understand) and language (especially poetry) point beyond themselves.

> To refuse to see in human desire an incompleteness that urges the soul on to transcendence is to remain within the realm of creatures, worshipping them as only the Creator was to be worshipped. Similarly, to refuse to see language and poetry as continual *askesis*, pointing beyond themselves, is to remain within the letter, treating it as an absolute devoid of the spirit which gives meaning to human discourse.[18]

A typological understanding of the relationship between the Old Testament and the New Testament is no longer limited to the figure of the veil that covered Moses' face and its antitype of Christ. This kind of interpretive relationship is extended to include Dante's life and conversion. It now includes the Medusa in the *Inferno* and the hermeneutic procedures of the revealing spirit. We can extend it further to texts such as Rousseau's *Discourses*, novels, and autobiography, which have seemed up to now to threaten a kind of spiritual petrification. They can be interpreted in such a way that they give life. Texts that are obstacles can become pathways to a deeper understanding of reality. Dante's poem delineates a hermeneutic that allows them to participate in the same kind of "retrospective illumination by faith."

The two different modes of interpretation, the letter that kills and the spirit that gives life, do not exactly face off with one another. Rather, the biblical tradition uses its literal understanding of an event both to subvert the dominant interpretation from within and to open itself to progressively deeper meanings. This is the import of the schema of allegorical interpretation developed in the Middle Ages, which reached its high point in the poetry of Dante. The letter that kills, an inherently violent interpretation,

corresponds to an assertion of meaning in which the literal meaning is true
and the figural meaning is not. It is the view of language and poetry that
Freccero described above: the refusal to see language or poetry as pointing
beyond itself. Remaining within the letter is form of idolatry. The biblical
model allows for a new hermeneutics that opens up figural interpretation.

To clarify this kind of interpretation, let us continue to take Dante as our
model. Dante gives us an example of how to read in his famous letter to Con
Grande, which functions as a kind of reflection upon his way of writing *The
Divine Comedy.*

> For me to be able to present what I am going to say, you must know that
> the sense of this work is not simple, rather it may be called polysemantic,
> that is, of many senses; the first sense is that which comes from the letter,
> the second is that which is signified by the letter. And the first is called the
> literal, the second allegorical or moral or anagogical. Which method of
> treatment, that it may be clearer, can be considered through these words:
> "When Israel went out of Egypt, the house of Jacob from a barbarous peo-
> ple, Judea was made his sanctuary, Israel his dominion" (Douay-Rheims,
> Ps. 113:1–2). If we look at it from the letter alone it means to us the exit of
> the Children of Israel from Egypt at the time of Moses; if from allegory,
> it means for us our redemption done by Christ; if from the moral sense, it
> means to us the conversion of the soul from the struggle and misery of sin
> to the status of grace; if from the anagogical, it means the leavetaking of the
> blessed soul from the slavery of this corruption to the freedom of eternal
> glory. And though these mystical senses are called by various names, in gen-
> eral all can be called allegorical, because they are different from the literal
> or the historical. Now, allegory comes from Greek *alleon*, which in Latin
> means *other* or *different.*[19]

Dante distinguishes, then, two senses of meaning with four possible modes of
interpretation: the literal and the figurative, with the figurative having three
subcategories. Dante's schema begins with the literal or historical level. In
this case it refers to the historical exodus of the Hebrew people from slavery
in Egypt to freedom in the Promised Land. But this literal or historical level
is not simply "given" to the poet or to the reader. This level too is an interpretation. Furthermore, the kind of literal or historical level that supports the

figurative involves a radically different kind of interpretation from the one imposed on the event by the dominant, persecuting power.

Accordingly, only a certain type of interpretation on this literal level can serve as the basis for the spiritual or figurative level. It is due to this kind of interpretation, projected backwards by the first Christians on the events of the Old Testament, that they became types for events in the New Testament, for the Church and for life of the individual Christian.[20]

Two Historical Readings

The example Dante used can be developed in order to clarify the way in which interpretation on the literal level affects everything that follows. One form of the interpretation of language and poetry sees them as directed toward a true transcendence, and another encases them within a false or deviated transcendence. The difference between these two modes ultimately rests on violence.

For example, Christians are quite used to reading and thinking about the Exodus story in the following way. After many plagues sent by God, including the death of the Pharoah's first-born son, the Pharaoh finally agreed to let the Hebrews leave Egypt. There are, though, good grounds for thinking that this is very much the story as told from the Israelites' perspective. From the Egyptians' vantage point, it may have been interpreted in the following way. Egypt was in crisis, besieged by plagues. Its people discovered that the culprits behind these plagues were the perfidious Hebrews, whom they then expelled into the desert. In other words, even on a literal or, in this case, historical level of what actually happened, there are implicitly two competing interpretations. As told from the viewpoint of the dominant power, the story of the Exodus becomes the story of the expulsion of the foreigner. The claim that Pharaoh, finally forced to agree to what YWHY wanted, freed God's people competes with the claim that Pharaoh expelled the foreigners. Both are interpretations, and both claim to be interpretations on a historical or literal level. There are, indeed, traces of them both in the text.

One cannot say that this violent act by the Pharaoh of expelling the Israelites is without its larger meanings, that it is absolutely devoid of transcendence. It is a political power-play with all that implies. One can claim, however, that the position of the dominant group as a literal position is closed to figural or allegorical meanings. It is locked into this world. The Israelites were expelled—end of story. Here history is closed in upon itself. On a literal level this interpretation is, without doubt, true. The act of expelling is an act of violence, and this makes the statement, "Pharaoh expelled the Hebrews," literally true. In fact, the violent act constitutes the truth of the interpretation. This is what Pharaoh did; this is what he intended; he imposed his will. Thus, the violent act can generate a meaning not lost on other oppressed groups. The Israelites were expelled, and through this expulsion order in society was restored.

The violent act (Pharaoh's expelling the Hebrews) and the nature of the order generated by it (Egyptian society is better off without foreigners) are analogous. Moreover, they are sacrificial in structure. The truth content of the sentences that express this act and this order might seem the same as that of the sentence, "When Israel went out of Egypt . . . ," but in fact these two interpretations are as structurally different as the violent act differs from the salvific and as the Egyptian social order differs from God's order. The difference lies in a truth or an order that is built on expulsion or exclusion versus one that is built on reintegrating that which was expelled. The former always rests upon some initial, violent negation. The latter, built on the subversion from within of the former order, does not depend on the expulsion of anything—not even of the order it is subverting.

The truth of the former is sacrificial in that it expels other possible meanings, as we shall see below. Something is expelled in order to structure that which remains, and that which remains is structured precisely around the absent victim. The Hebrews became scapegoats in order to promote social cohesion among the ruling class. At the same time, the persecutors' viewpoint imposes itself *to the exclusion* of the victims' viewpoint. The sentence, "Egypt expelled the Hebrews," is factually correct but so limited in its perspective as to be, finally, historically wrong. The sentence reveals, notwithstanding its declarative intent, how the logic of sacrifice is caught up in the arbitrariness of violence. Yet it is also true that the act's violence can be mesmerizing, so scandalous that the literal interpretation petrifies the mind and blocks any deeper understanding.

If the literal interpretation of the Exodus is that Pharaoh expelled the Hebrews, this seems to exclude the interpretation that YWHY freed them. The event of their expulsion, however, could be experienced in another way.

The true transcendence of Moses was to prepare his people for this event. The Egyptians would claim that the Hebrews were being expelled into the desert, the place of death, but Moses told them that their God was the God of the desert and that He was arranging for them to be freed.

When such an event is interpreted by the logic of sacrifice, the connection between the representation in language (e.g., "Pharaoh expelled the Hebrews) and the referent (the Exodus) is a reified one in which the words used to name the event get closed off from other possible meanings. This leads to the loss of meaning that we examined in the first chapter. Who would remember the Exodus if all it involved was the expulsion of a minority by a dominant power? On the other hand, the interpretation that God intervened through Moses gives the event a literally new, multidimensional meaning.

In this way the event is interpreted as being not sacrificial but salvific. God saves His people, and through this action they become precisely that. The words of the story begin to refer not only to the historical event but also to a multiplicity of realities, the meanings of which deepen and broaden. Words become part of the realities to which they refer, and this kind of union becomes mutually enriching. Exodus becomes a symbol that many groups have used to express their own hopes and dreams. During the demonstrations of 2011 in Egypt that brought down its government, a sign was seen in Tahrir Square that read, "If Mubarak is Pharaoh, then we are all Moses."

The Judeo-Christian Scriptures offer a new and open *literal* interpretation of particular violent events in history. In the example given, the Hebrew people are substituted for—that is, they become the sign of the plagues that are afflicting Egypt. The persecutors expelled them in an attempt to rid Egypt of its woes. Moses, however, offers another interpretation. He sees the event as God's deliverance of His people. The two possible literal interpretations—that Pharaoh expelled the Hebrews and that God saved his people—read as the letter that kills versus the spirit that gives life. This point could be construed as indicating two competing interpretations of the same event more or less on the same level, but this is not true. The newness of the Judeo-Christian reading is that in a certain sense it presumes a sacrificial reading of a violent event. When Paul writes, "For the letter kills, but the spirit gives life" (1Cor. 3:6), he does not suggest expelling the letter. Rather, the spirit is such that it allows the same that was lethal now to confer life. A *new* covenant fulfills the old one.

This tradition can acknowledge Pharaoh's understanding of the Exodus, even as it gives it a new literal meaning. The dominant group's interpretation contributes to the reality that is being interpreted. The Pharaoh, in order to sustain his own sacrificial interpretation, is forced to reject the other literal interpretation, but Moses' view does not oppose the Pharaoh's in this way. Moses can allow the Pharaoh's view to stand and even insist upon it. It is the violent situation into which God's peace is going to erupt. Since Moses' view is not locked into an opposition with Pharaoh's in the way that Pharaoh's is with Moses,' the former has the openness to more interpretations and meanings. The relationship between the sign and its referent is not sacrificial; this form of interpretation allows the word, the story, to become part of the reality it expresses. It allows the story to have other referents.

From the Exodus to the Passion

A common understanding regarding Jesus' death is expressed in the Christian narrative of redemption. It goes something like the following: God created a good world.[21] Humans then chose to sin, thereby separating themselves from God and incurring His wrath. Jesus Christ ransomed us by dying on the cross, thereby placating God. This is a caricature but not a distortion.

The problem with this approach of identifying first the problem, namely sin, and then the solution, redemption through the cross, is that it presumes we have some sort of independent epistemological access to sin, or into what the true state of our human condition without God could be. I do not mean to imply that only Christians have a sense of the ethical or the moral. Humans have a sense of right and wrong. Still, *sin* is only revealed for what it truly is in light of God's love and forgiveness. We have no way of getting to anything resembling the doctrine of Original Sin without the cross. The crucifixion of Christ reveals what sin at its core is. First, then, is the Christ-event, and through that we understand what it was from which we were saved. This puts the victim of violence and his forgiveness, at the center of Christian faith. It puts the problem of violence and our participation in it at the center of our problems, personal and communal.

Allegorical meaning opens up more than levels of meaning. It is only in light of allegory that we will be able to understand the change in meaning that Christianity has wrought in violent situations. It offers, as I have shown, the possibility of a new literal interpretation. Further, only in terms of allegory can we begin to overcome the loss of meaning in language as pointed out in the first chapter. Events themselves and the words used to represent them take on deeper meaning rather than being emptied out. Finally, only in this way can we understand the monumental shift that has occurred between Plato, who urged us to control the desire to look at the corpses, and Danner, who sees this looking as the best way to arrive at deeper meanings. The "portal" through which Danner sees the executed corpses was opened by Christ. The violent interpretation of Jesus of Nazareth's death is that a troublemaker and seditious person has been put to death according to Roman law and in accordance with God's wishes. The Christian interpretation is that God's own Son and a righteous man has been put to death by other human beings. Paul inscribes the received tradition: "that Christ died for our sins in accordance with the scriptures, and that he was buried, and that he was raised on the third day in accordance with the scriptures" (1Cor. 15:3). This is not a reference to some particular passage or set of passages in the Old Testament. It refers instead to the inner logic of the Scriptures. It involves a rereading of the Hebrew Scriptures. What the Scriptures tell us is that Christ had to be killed, not because God wanted it but because humans are that way. Christ had to be raised on the third day to redeem us from what the Crucifixion had revealed about us.

Even within the Gospel these two interpretations are so arranged that the second subverts the first. Read in one way Caiaphas, the high priest, spoke the logic that has grounded the world since its inception: "It is better for you to have one man die for the people than to have the whole nation destroyed" (John 11:50). Read in another way, this "prophecy" posits that Jesus died not only for the nation but to "gather into one the dispersed children of God" (John 11:52). Because this death will reveal the sacrificial mechanism that gathers only to disperse and disperses only to gather, it will be a definitive gathering of God's dispersed children.

Presenting the Passion story from the point of view of the victim reveals not just a new interpretation but a new rationality that comprehends the old model.[22] It can, but it does not have to. We see the internal tension between the appearance of salvation in the person of Jesus and the preparation for that appearance in the person of John the Baptist as well as in the reaction of the Scribes and Pharisees. The tension suggests that, no matter how deep or comprehensive the preparation has been, there always remains a scandal to be overcome. The Scribes and Pharisees accused Jesus of destroying the true religion, of uprooting the traditions and of violently making himself equal to God. For his part, John the Baptist, after he had been imprisoned, sent two of his followers to ask Jesus whether he was the "one" or whether they should wait for another. The question itself suggests that there were things in Jesus' message and behavior that raised painful questions for John about his own identification of Jesus as the "one who is to come." Jesus replied, "Tell John what you have seen and what you have heard. The blind see, the lame walk, lepers are cleansed and the poor have the Good News preached to them" (Matt. 11:4–5). There is no violence in this interpretation. We cannot simply conclude that the New Testament presents the reader with another "conflict of interpretations," meaning that one interpretation would be as good as another. Jesus himself, in his final comment to John, undercuts this possibility when he says, "Blessed is he who is not scandalized in me" (Matt. 11:6). He means that, rather than a conflict of interpretations, his own actions are the true fulfillment of the very religious tradition he is accused of trying to destroy. If John is looking for a Messiah, he must be willing to see the whole thing from a new perspective. It is not one claim to being Messiah versus another. In fact, Jesus deliberately does not make that claim precisely to avoid this kind of conflict. He does not insist, and he does not impose. He loves; he forgives; he heals. Some followers, though, saw Jesus of Nazareth as innocent and as hated without cause. They saw in him the fulfillment of their religion and the Savior of their people. The proof of this was the Resurrection. He was truly accursed by humans, yet he saved the community. He showed that God is not responsible for human violence, no matter how much we try to make it respectable by divinizing it.

"Tell John what you have seen and what you have heard." The activities and the teachings of Jesus may not impose an interpretation, but they do present a clear option. Either the whole tradition was leading up to Jesus as its fulfillment, or it was not. There is no third option. The work of Jesus, considered as the Messiah, is a scandal, and one has to choose not to be scandalized but to believe.[23]

CHAPTER 5

The Lesson of the Gospels

Beyond Scandal?

Plato understood the limitations of reason. Reason cannot, on its own, withstand the temptation of looking at corpses. For that, Plato enlists another part of the soul, the spirited part with its anger. Anger does not enable one to look at the victim; instead, it keeps one's gaze steady as one walks by the spectacle. The spirited part of the soul plays a role, as we shall see, analogous to that of primitive religion. Religion, in its traditional role, allows one to walk past the victim; in other words, it hides the victim.

In this sense Rousseau and Nietzsche were the last true Platonists. For Nietzsche it is art rather than religion that keeps the gaze steadily averted from the victim. Art performs a kind of alchemy in transforming the victim from a portal to deeper anthropological knowledge to a spectacle that arrests the eyes and keeps them fascinated. Rousseau also wants the reader to look without seeing and to listen without understanding. He scandalizes the reader in order to fascinate, keeping her entrapped in a cycle of attraction and repulsion. For Rousseau the victim will always be only Rousseau himself, and the persecutor will always be the other. The reader, on the other hand, will oscillate between these two positions: the victim in the center or the persecutor on the periphery.[1] Rousseau's art never allows us to stay in either of these positions long enough to understand it. We are constantly being shocked, fascinated, and scandalized by either Rousseau or his authorial projection.

A scandalized consciousness cannot escape or overcome scandal. The very attempt to do so further enmeshes one in it. How, then, does one escape the world of scandal? Is there an alternative? I offer below some suggestions about how to read scandalous texts from the Gospels.

The Stone

The women heading toward the tomb of Jesus were preoccupied with an obstacle they feared would interfere with their task of anointing Jesus' corpse. They asked each other, "Who will roll away the stone for us from the entrance to the tomb?" (Mark 16:3) Their fears, as it turned out, were needless: the stone had already been rolled away. That obstacle removed, a more difficult one appeared, and a greater fear emerged. The tomb was empty; there was no body to anoint. Instead, there was a young man who announced, "he has been raised; he is not here. Look, there is the place they laid him" (Mark 16:6). This chapter seeks in some small way to duplicate in the reader the experience of these women. It attempts to make explicit the obstacles that we believe we face in reading texts. Using some Gospel texts, I raise some issues and problems in order to get the reader to pose the question, "Who will roll away the stone for us from the entrance of the tomb?" Then, hopefully, a moment will come when the reader understands that the stone has already been removed. The immediate relief of the open tomb should then be followed by a trembling at its emptiness.

The issues and problems that I raise with these texts are not pseudo-problems. Before the women saw that the stone had been removed, it was natural for them to be concerned about it. So the women were not "wrong" to go to the tomb, nor were they "wrong" to be concerned about how they would get inside it. In light of the Resurrection, however, these acts become way stations to revelation of the true task. The real obstacle turns out not to be an obstacle at all. The empty tomb reveals the need for faith and indicates to the women what they are to do—proclaim the resurrected Lord.

Thus, the texts indicate an obstacle that is not an obstacle at all. It in fact has characteristics that are the opposite of those of the stone: rather than blocking the way, this obstacle is *nothing*. The tomb is empty, yet it poses an obstacle to human understanding. What can the empty tomb mean? *He* is not there. That is all that the women can see. Hence, they are bewildered; they flee; they say nothing.

The empty tomb scandalized the women. This scandal led them to faith and the ability to proclaim to the disciples where the risen Lord was. Where this deeper scandal will lead the present-day reader is not for me to say. I will have accomplished my task if I can move the reader beyond the preliminary scandal at the stone to the deeper scandal of the empty tomb. My role corresponds roughly to that of the young man in the tomb pointing to the obvious: "He is not here."

The Call of Matthew

Jesus' call of Matthew sketches in broad outline the movement of the whole Bible: a movement away from sacrifice and toward mercy or love. The paradigmatic genre of Gospel writing, the parable, will demonstrate how it both scandalizes and delivers the reader from scandal. Finally, some considerations of the "spiritual" life will show how it can help someone read texts without being scandalized.

Matthew recounts his own call by Jesus. Matthew was one of the "sinners," one of those whom, by their occupation and by the place in which they sat (the tax collector's booth), everyone, including himself, knew to be a sinner. While he was occupying this place of shame,[2] Jesus came up to him and said, "Follow me" (Matt. 9:9). That evening Matthew celebrated this call and invited his fellow tax collectors to join Jesus and his other disciples. When the Pharisees saw this, they asked the disciples, "Why does your teacher eat with tax collectors and sinners?" (Matt. 9:11).

The question indicates that the Pharisees were scandalized by Jesus' behavior. Jesus had called as his disciple a tax collector; he was associating with people who were unclean, people who were not good because of their dealings with pagan overlords. Jesus overheard the Pharisees' question and said, in effect, 'You would not yet understand the answer to your own question.' His actual words were: "Those who are well have no need of a physician, but those who are sick. Go and learn what this means, 'I desire mercy not sacrifice.' For I have come to call not the righteous but sinners" (Matt. 9:12–13, with Jesus quoting Hos. 6:6).

It is certainly correct to read this passage as indicating that the Pharisees should stop worrying about who is righteous and instead extend merciful compassion to the people whom they are judging so harshly. There is a need for caution, however. While one can see a connection between the sick and sinners and between the well and the righteous, it is not clear what sacrifice has to do with all this. The Pharisees are asking why Jesus is eating with sinners, not why the sinners aren't offering more sacrifices. Further, this reading can shift all too easily away from what is going on in the story—namely, a condemnation by the Pharisees of Jesus for associating with people whom they have already condemned, to a condemnation by the reader of the Pharisees and their attitude. The only difference is that, while the Pharisees' condemnation of the tax collectors and sinners is criticized by Jesus, the reader's condemnation of the Pharisees seems sanctioned by him.

Jesus' answer to the Pharisees' question seems to follow a certain logic that we can summarize as follows: just as there are sick people who need a doctor, so there are sinners who need the mercy that God desires humans to practice, and so these sinners, like Matthew, are being called. Jesus is doing what God desires in calling the sinners. Moreover, this logic entails polar opposites: the sick, the sinners, and mercy on the one hand; the healthy, the righteous, and sacrifice on the other. So just as the healthy do not need a doctor, the righteous do not need mercy but do practice sacrifice. This leads, of course, to the paradoxical conclusion that it is actually the righteous who are both doing what God does not want and are not being called.

In fact, this is not quite the logic of the passage, although it is close. And, as is so often the case with the Gospels, to be nearly right is to be very wrong.[3] The logic above understands Jesus as saying, "God desires mercy and not sacrifice; therefore, I have (mercifully) come to call sinners." The prophet's words thus become a kind of warrant to show that in associating with sinners Jesus is doing God's will. This may well be true, but what Jesus actually says is that, *because* I am calling sinners, you, the Pharisees, must learn the meaning of the words, 'I desire mercy, not sacrifice.' It is not because God desires mercy that Jesus is mercifully calling sinners; instead, because he is calling sinners, the Pharisees have to learn the true meaning of God's desires. Jesus is not justifying his own actions to the Pharisees but trying to get them to see the Hebrew Scriptures in their proper light.

The Pharisees are commanded to "Go and learn the meaning. . . ." They are, that is, to undertake a journey of interpretation. This suggests that the meaning of the words quoted is not obvious. Out of all the quotations from the prophets that Jesus could have chosen to respond to the Pharisees' question, why did he choose one that expressly opposes merciful compassion to ritual sacrifice? Why is it these words that the Pharisees have to understand? The Pharisees were not insisting on the offering of sacrifice, and no one was agitating against it. The controversy was about the people with whom Jesus was associating.

The Pharisees were offended at Jesus' behavior of sitting at a table with tax collectors and sinners. This was their initial offense, and Jesus simply said to them, 'Think about it for one second: sick people need a doctor, not healthy ones. So if these people are sick, as you seem to think, then I go among them to heal them. No one would criticize a doctor for being with sick people, so don't criticize me for being with so-called sinners.' Their initial scandal evaporated. Then Jesus revealed the deeper, truer scandal. He was not just eating with sinners; he was calling them to be followers.

This must have struck the Pharisees as perverse, and we can understand why. If Jesus' mission was, as he proclaimed, not to abrogate the Law but to fulfill it, why would he call those who were furthest away from the Law rather than those who, while not perfect, were at least further along in keeping the Law? Unless, of course, the fulfillment of the Law lay precisely in the inclusion of those who were furthest away.

It is the call of sinners and its relation to the abrogation of sacrifice that comprise the scandal of this passage. Why does the call of sinners necessitate an understanding of the words, 'I desire mercy, not sacrifice'? How is the offense at Jesus' calling sinners related to thinking that God desires sacrifice? Turning this around, how will the Pharisees be freed from their offense by understanding that God does not desire sacrifice but instead mercy? This ultimately is what is demanded of the Pharisees—not some notional assent to the superiority of love over ritual but a real assent in their hearts and minds to fellowship with sinners. Apparently this kind of assent was possible only if their understanding of God changed.

The logic of Jesus' words holds that, because he calls sinners, the Pharisees must learn the meaning of Hosea's words about the priority of mercy over sacrifice. The act of calling sinners is the portal to understanding a God who desires love rather than burnt offerings. The practice of Jesus becomes the measure by which we are to understand the meaning of the prophecy, and the prophecy helps us to understand his practice. The calling of sinners to discipleship is the mercy that God desires. In this way Jesus gives a concrete shape to the definitions of sinner and mercy. It is not so much that one must be an obvious sinner—a tax collector such as Matthew—to be called, but rather that by being called and forgiven people are fully constituted as sinners. To be called is to be a sinner; conversely, to be truly a sinner is to be called. This is the meaning of Peter's reaction to the huge catch of fish when Jesus called him: "Go away from me, Lord, for I am a sinful man!" (Luke 5:8). In other words, Jesus doesn't call because one is a sinner and therefore has a certain claim to be called; instead, his call includes God's love and forgiveness so that the person called becomes a forgiven sinner. And this then is what mercy becomes: extending forgiving fellowship to those regarded by others as sinners.

This brings us to the nucleus of the Pharisees' scandal. Jesus' action threatens to reveal that God is not who they think he is and that the world is not ordered according to their preconception of it. Jesus does not call the righteous, and God does not desire sacrifice. Jesus has drawn a connection between the Pharisees' lack of understanding desire, compassion, and sacrifice and their lack of understanding his actions. He suggests that their trust in sacrifice is related to their confidence in labeling certain people sinners. If the Pharisees can grasp that God does not desire sacrifice but mercy, perhaps they also will be able to grasp that labeling someone a sinner is beyond their competence.

More accurately, if the Pharisees are, as the passage implies, basically ignorant about the nature of God's desire, perhaps they are mistaken also about righteousness and sin.[4] A change in their understanding would imply a change in their status. It is possible that they would come to see themselves as sinners, at one with Matthew and his friends. Then they would also be the object of Jesus' call, and this Gospel would turn out to be good news for them also.

When Jesus commands the Pharisees to "go," where is he directing them? How are they to learn? They are being told that, in order to answer their own question about why Jesus eats with sinners, they have to get over their initial scandal and enter into a greater scandal. They must understand that not only does he eat with sinners but that he also calls them. Then they have to allow the meaning of the words "I desire mercy, not sacrifice" to be revealed to them in all their fullness. Jesus' behavior appears scandalous to them *because* they have read the Hebrew Scriptures, so now they need to reread them in order to find a new meaning. They thought they knew what those Scriptures meant; Jesus is telling them that they were mistaken. Thus, to learn what the words "I desire mercy, not sacrifice" mean is to reread the Scriptures in a certain way. More than that, it is to see the reality of Jesus' behavior and people such as Matthew in a new light.

We are given another angle from which to view the issues involved in learning to reread. In what I believe is a unique instance in the New Testament, Matthew has Jesus re-use the same quotation from Hosea just a few pages after the passage we have been considering. In chapter 12, Jesus and his disciples walk through fields on the Sabbath, and his disciples pluck heads of grain intending to eat them. In a way that parallels the earlier passage, the Pharisees are offended by this behavior and voice their condemnation: "Look, your disciples are doing what is not lawful to do on the Sabbath." In response Jesus asks, "Have you not read what David did when he and his companions were hungry? . . . Or have you not read in the law that on the Sabbath the priests in the temple break the Sabbath and yet are guiltless?" Of course, the Pharisees have read the account. The complaint and the response echo chapter 9 but also point to a difference. The Pharisees' earlier offense was about something in the secular realm—eating a meal. Here we are much more directly concerned with the sacred. The disciples are breaking the Sabbath. Jesus' response is not an appeal to a "secular" truth about doctors and the sick but a challenge regarding how the Pharisees understand the sacred text. The issues go directly to the Temple, the sacred place of sacrifice, and to lordship over the Sabbath.

This time the logic in Jesus' appeal to the words of Hosea is more straightforward and therefore more mysterious. He says, "But if you had known what this means, 'I desire mercy and not sacrifice,' you would not have condemned the guiltless." That is, Jesus draws a clear causal link between their misunderstanding of those words and their condemnation of the "guiltless." He does not dispute what the disciples are doing; he disputes the Pharisees' interpretation of it. He says that because they envision God as desiring sacrifice, and because they themselves desire sacrifice, they are compelled to condemn the guiltless. If they could enter into an understanding of the words, "I desire mercy and not sacrifice," their scandal would disappear. Jesus seems again to go out of his way to use the quotation from Hosea without using indirect discourse, thereby emphasizing the "I" in "I desire mercy and not sacrifice" rather than saying that God desires mercy. He does this in part to make this desire his own and, further, to indicate that each person must be able to say '*I* understand the meaning of the words, "*I* desire mercy and not sacrifice."'

If Matthew is sending the reader on a journey of interpretation within his own Gospel, the hope is that, unlike the Pharisees who do not make any progress from one occurrence of the words of Hosea to the next, the reader will begin to pick up clues for a new understanding. The intervening text is filled with instances of Jesus doing things similar to eating with sinners or his disciples doing what is unlawful on the Sabbath. Out of all the incidents, I want to draw attention to one somewhat odd juxtaposition that cannot have been accidental.

Right after Jesus says that he calls sinners, the disciples of John the Baptist come to him with a question: "Are you the one who is to come, or are we to wait for another?" (Matt. 11:3). John in Matthew's Gospel represents the whole of Israel's salvation history. I do not think that John's temptation to be scandalized by Jesus was all that different from the scandal that the Pharisees actually took at Jesus. Let us try to understand John's situation more deeply. Herod had arrested and imprisoned him. While in prison John heard what Christ was doing. He then sent his disciples with his question.

When someone is incarcerated, he has time to reflect on the events that brought him there. The works produced by Dietrich Bonhoeffer, Alfred Delp, Alexander Solzhenitsyn, Mahatma Gandhi, and Martin Luther King testify to the clarity of thought that can be born inside prison walls. John the Baptist was arrested and imprisoned by Herod because he had criticized Herod for marrying his brother's wife. John was scandalized by the acts of a scandalous court, and now he was suffering the consequences. In this state he heard "what the Messiah was doing" (Matt. 11:2). Something in what he heard disturbed him deeply enough to question an identification he had made on the occasion of Jesus' baptism. When Jesus had presented himself to be baptized, John had demurred: "I need to be baptized by you, and do you come to me" (Matt. 3:13). John proclaimed this person to be the one for whom he had been preparing the way, but now in prison John seemed to be questioning his whole life's work. Are you really the one, or was I wrong? You are supposed to be baptizing with the Holy Spirit and with fire. You are to be clearing the threshing floor, gathering the wheat, and burning up the chaff with unquenchable fire (see Matt. 3:12).

I think that Jesus understood every nuance to the question that John's disciples put to him: "Are you the one who is to come, or should we expect another?" Jesus' answer is both respectful and challenging. "Go and tell John," he declared, "what you hear and see: the blind receive sight, the lame walk, the lepers are cleansed, the deaf hear, the dead are raised, and the poor have good news preached to them" (Matt. 11:4–5). Jesus put his strongest credentials before John to prove that he was God's anointed, the one who fulfills everything that the Law and the Prophets had prophesied. Jesus then formulated a new beatitude: "Blessed is whoever is not scandalized in me" (Matt. 11:6).[5]

Jesus admitted what Paul later proclaims: he can become a stumbling block, a cause of sin, to those who approach him. By addressing this particular beatitude to John the Baptist, Jesus suggests that the closer one is to him (John the Baptist is the only person recorded in the New Testament to take the title of "friend" in reference to Jesus [John 3:29]), the more susceptible one is to scandal. We see this also in the case of Peter. Blessed, then, is the one who does not stumble on account of Jesus. In effect, if you do not fall away because of Jesus, you will not fall away at all. One can fall away through concern over material comfort and reputation, but even if one has conquered these, there remains the danger of falling away because of Christ himself. If one does not fall away on account of him, one is truly blessed.

We have to assume that we have been given enough information in the story to understand what scandalized John. The interplay between John's query and Christ's answer provides us with an insight into what can cause stumbling. The question John posed is not an academic or objective one. I think that we are on the right track to read it in the following way: 'Is this, what I hear you are doing, what salvation looks like? Is this how God comes to save His people—to save me?' John had a set of expectations that were formed by his religion. Jesus confronted John with something which differed from these. And then he promised beatitude.

If the life and death of Jesus have scandal as a constitutive element, how and why is somebody who finds no scandal there blessed? Jesus is suggesting 'Precisely insofar as you draw close to me, you will be tempted to stumble. My relationship with you will inevitably lead to that point where you do not want to go, where you will find it difficult to follow. I will ask something of you that you would rather not give. It will be particular to who you are, the thing to which you are attached.' For John the Baptist it was his own vision of the Messiah. In effect, John the Baptist faced the same challenge as the Pharisees—getting beneath the surface of the "strange verses" to the true doctrine.

"Blessed is whoever is not scandalized in me." In Luke's version of the beatitudes we find four beatitudes balanced with four woes. 'Blessed are the poor.—Woe to the rich. Blessed are the hungry.—Woe to the well-fed. Blessed are those who weep.—Woe to those who laugh. Blessed are you when others hate, exclude, insult, and reject you.—Woe to those who are well regarded.' In light of this structure it would seem that the parallel woe to the new beatitude is 'Woe to him who is scandalized in me,' but we never read those words. Instead, we read warnings against scandalizing others. Why is that? I want to show that being scandalized by Christ and causing scandal to others are not, in the end, two different realities. We are blessed if we are not scandalized in Christ because then we will not be scandalized by anything. He is truly scandalous, yet we are not scandalized; and since we no long live in the world of scandal, we no longer scandalize others.

This does not mean that others are not scandalized. Christ *is* a scandal. Does that mean that Christ breaks his own prohibition against causing scandal? By no means, as Paul might say. He cannot be without scandal, and the Gospel cannot be proclaimed without the element of scandal. Still, blessed are those who find no scandal in him. When we follow him without stumbling, we become the same sort of model for others that he is to us—a perpetual stumbling block that the blessed do not stumble over.

The Pharisees were offended at Jesus' fraternizing with sinners, and in response Jesus sent them on a journey of understanding. By and large modern readers are not offended at Jesus' behavior. He can eat with whomever he pleases, as far as we are concerned. We do not need to wish to return to a culture that regarded some people as "unclean" in order that we might appreciate the Gospel's meaning. Our own offense at the Pharisees' attitude toward Jesus and sinners is enough. If we find their attitude objectionable, that will suffice. If we condemn them as sinners, that will do. Yet, if this is our response, then we too must embark on the journey of learning what these words mean: "I desire mercy, not sacrifice."

We can get beneath the surface of the text by asking the following questions. What is it to desire sacrifice? Why do we think that God desires sacrifice? How does a desire for sacrifice or an understanding of God as desiring sacrifice lead to a belief that the righteous are the ones called? Is the desire for sacrifice based on a distinction between the righteous and sinners, or is that distinction ultimately based on sacrifice?

The Pharisees confrontations with Jesus over his eating with sinners and over his disciples behavior on the Sabbath both suggest that their default position was an expectation that the righteous will be called and not sinners, that they were offended when this expectation was not met, and that this default position was connected with another by which sacrifice was seen as something desirable. Jesus enjoined them to cease seeing God as desirous of sacrifice and instead see Him as desirous of mercy. This would lead them to accept the practice of calling sinners and not the righteous, as well as to see themselves as sinners (sacrificers) in need of forgiveness.

The previous chapter showed that the Scriptures can reveal new, peaceful possibilities inherent in violent situations like the Exodus. These new interpretations, as recorded in the Scriptures or in Dante, do not emerge of themselves; instead, they get incarnated, individually and collectively, by people creating new forms of life.

This fact gives us a way to think about being "spiritual" or "religious" in the twenty-first century. Earlier I noted that Christ's crucifixion and resurrection reveals both the essence and the dimensions of sin. We have to begin with the Christ-event, with salvation, and through it we understand that from which we are being saved. Thus, the forgiving victim stands at the center of Christian faith. This victim is a victim of violence and so his centrality suggests that violence is an essential part of our understanding of sin, both personal and communal. I would add, too, that it puts our belonging in a violent and sacrificial way to groups at the center. This is the way we learn to see ourselves as part of the mob. To ground this claim and to show that the victim is the center and measure of our spirituality, I offer the following understanding of parables, doctrines, and rituals.

Parables

I begin with the Gospel of Mark's version of the Parable of the Sower, along
with the disciples' request for its meaning and Jesus' own interpretation.
There are several things to note before reading it. First, it is one of the few
parables for which Jesus himself is credited with providing an interpretation.
Second, it is clear from the parable's placement in the text and its content
that it is meant to provide a key for helping the reader understand all the
parables. Finally, of all genres, the parable is the one most closely linked to
Jesus' teaching. The Kingdom of God that he proclaimed seems only to be
able to be understood though parables. Understanding the logic of parables
will help us to understand the logic of the Kingdom and, indeed, the logic
of the Scriptures.

Now let us read the Parable of the Sower in Mark's fourth chapter.

Again he began to teach beside the sea. Such a very large crowd gathered
around him that he got into a boat on the sea and sat there, while the whole
crowd was beside the sea on the land. [2]He began to teach them many things
in parables, and in his teaching he said to them: [3]"Listen! A sower went out
to sow. [4]And as he sowed, some seed fell on the path, and the birds came
and ate it up. [5]Other seed fell on rocky ground, where it did not have much
soil, and it sprang up quickly, since it had no depth of soil. [6]And when
the sun rose, it was scorched; and since it had no root, it withered away.
[7]Other seed fell among thorns, and the thorns grew up and choked it, and
it yielded no grain.[8]Other seed fell into good soil and brought forth grain,
growing up and increasing and yielding thirty and sixty and a hundred-
fold." [9]And he said, "Let anyone with ears to hear listen!"

[10]When he was alone, those who were around him along with the
twelve asked him about the parables. [11]And he said to them, "To you has
been given the secret of the kingdom of God, but for those outside, everything comes in parables; [12]in order that

'they may indeed look, but not perceive,

and may indeed listen, but not understand;

so that they may not turn again and be forgiven.'"

[13]And he said to them, "Do you not understand this parable? Then

how will you understand all the parables? [14]The sower sows the word. [15]These are the ones on the path where the word is sown: when they hear, Satan immediately comes and takes away the word that is sown in them. [16]And these are the ones sown on rocky ground: when they hear the word, they immediately receive it with joy. [17]But they have no root, and endure only for a while; then, when trouble or persecution arises on account of the word, immediately they fall away. [18]And others are those sown among the thorns: these are the ones who hear the word, [19]but the cares of the world, and the lure of wealth, and the desire for other things come in and choke the word, and it yields nothing. [20]And these are the ones sown on the good soil: they hear the word and accept it and bear fruit, thirty and sixty and a hundredfold."

The structure of this passage is a variation on a typical one that Mark often uses: a single story or event gets interrupted by another story or event before the original is concluded. In this case Mark inserts a dialogue between Jesus and his disciples that occasions the proffered interpretation. Still, the dialogue does not seem to add anything of substance to the interpretation or to give any clue about how one is to read parables in general. The dialogue has vexed many commentators because it clearly says that to those on the "outside" things will be spoken only in parables "in order that 'they may indeed look, . . . and may indeed listen, but not understand; so that they may not turn again and be forgiven.'" The immediate sense of this part of the parable is that, if one is not a member of the inner circle where a code is spoken, one will not be able to get "inside." Of course, this too is scandalous.

Frank Kermode does a wonderful job in *The Genesis of Secrecy* of pointing out the ways that this text has scandalized modern commentators. He begins simply by saying that the whole parable, including its interlude and interpretation, "is very odd."[6] The interpretation offered by Jesus seems strange in that the Word of God is the seed producing kinds of people. He points out how much scholarly energy has been expended to explain Mark's use of *hina*, translated above as "so that" as in "so that 'they may perceive but not understand.'" Kermode quotes commentators to the effect that this doctrine is "intolerable," "repellent," and "also, since the meaning of the parables is 'clear as day,' unintelligible."[7]

Indeed, as Kermode points out, Matthew replaces *hina* with *hoti*—that is, he replaces "so that" with "because." Matthew thereby substantially changes the meaning to a kind of ironic statement to the effect that 'the people are so dense that parables seem to be the only way to get through to them.' This emendation shifts the burden of the lack of intelligibility from Jesus' intention to the hearers' stupidity.

What Kermode makes clear is how certain assumptions such as "Jesus could not possibly have thought of his parables as riddles designed to exclude the masses from the kingdom" force one to claim that the "whole Marcan passage is unauthentic or corrupt."[8] Kermode is more comfortable with simply being in the dark as to the Parable of the Sower's meaning. His final comment is that "The riddle remains dark; so does the gospel."[9] I think, however, that more can be said.

Rousseau held that anything in the Gospel that offends reason, that seems to make God appear unjust to us has to be rejected as unworthy of the Scriptures.[10] This parable would fall under his scalpel. But the parable sits there in the text, like a boulder in our path. The more we try to get around it, the more it blocks our way. It has obviously disturbed commentators, as the above quotes show. Is there a way to "read" the parable?

The parable is typical for Jesus. It is agricultural; it is realistic; and yet it demands to be interpreted. Representing the Kingdom of God as a field that is sown and comparing the Kingdom's growth to that of a plant are both commonplaces in the Gospels. In this particular parable the seed sown is the Word of God. The soil upon which it lands represents the hearts of the people who hear this Word. According to the immediate sense of Jesus' interpretation of his own parable, we can say that there two basic classes of people: those who hear the Word, receive it, and bear fruit; and those who hear it and for whatever reason do not bear fruit. We can offer as a preliminary speculation that those who bear fruit are the ones on the "inside" who have received the secret of the Kingdom, while those who are barren correspond to people on the "outside" who get only parables.

Each of these two classes can be subdivided. Among those in whom the Word comes to fruition are varying degrees of fruitfulness. Jesus does not specify how the fruitfulness is to be measured, but I think it safe to assume that those who bear a hundred-fold are the people we call saints—that is, privileged souls who excel in the practice of faith, hope, and charity. The sixty-fold are somehow less exercised in these theological virtues, and the thirty-fold are regular believers. I will not repeat the various classes of those who do not bear fruit since their description is quite clear. According to this parable, then, we have world that is divided between those who bear fruit and those who do not, between those on the inside and those on the outside. While all this may seem plausible, I believe it is a serious misinterpretation. We do not need the Gospels to describe that kind of a world, which is one we inhabit by default.

The key to understanding how to interpret the parable lies in the dialogue between Christ and his disciples, which forms both an obstacle and a bridge between the parable and its interpretation. The disciples come to Jesus because they do not understand the parable. Thus, understanding or not understanding the parable cannot be the difference between those on the outside and those on the inside. The disciples have received the key to the Kingdom of Heaven without having understood anything. It is also important to note that Christ *never* speaks about those on the inside. There is no corresponding group of insiders versus outsiders. Who, then, are the poor people on the outside who will never convert? Understanding the difference between these groups will help us to understand those who respond to the Word of God fruitfully and those who do not.

Who are those on the outside? If we bring together everything we have discussed so far—the fact that understanding the parable is not the criterion, that Jesus never speaks about insiders, that Jesus calls the marginalized sinners—then our conclusion has to be that that those on the outside are the people who think that there is an inside and an outside. This is why Jesus never speaks of insiders. Those who are looking for a way to distinguish themselves from others, those who view the world as ordered between two groups (them and us)—represent precisely the kind of binary or polarized thinking that Jesus came to overcome. His disciples had received this "secret" of the Kingdom: there is no inside or outside—no in-group and no out-group. Both, in Jesus' interpretation of the parable, have to be seen as part of the Church. Luke offers an instructive lesson in this process with his famous parable of the Good Samaritan.

The Parable of the Good Samaritan

The story of the Good Samaritan is introduced by Jesus' encounter with a "lawyer," someone like a Pharisee, an expert in the Law of Moses. This lawyer "tests" Jesus by asking him a question: "What must I do to inherit eternal life?" Jesus does not give him a direct answer. Instead, he asks the lawyer to tell him exactly what he ought to know: "What is written in the law? *How do you read?* [translation modified]" The lawyer responds that he reads Scripture as saying that one is commanded to love God and one's neighbor as oneself. And Jesus tells him that he has answered correctly: "Do this, and you will live" (Luke 10:28). But the lawyer is not satisfied and wishes to "justify" himself, so he asks Jesus, "And who is my neighbor?" The parable of the Good Samaritan is Jesus' answer to that question.

Let us pause here to take our bearings. Until this parable's introduction, Luke has been following Mark's Gospel. In Mark, a scribe rather than a lawyer, a writer rather than a reader, comes to Jesus and asks, "Which commandment is the first of all?" (Mark 12:28). Jesus answers him directly, giving him the same answer as in the Lucan version. The scribe approves of Jesus' response and repeats it almost verbatim, but then he adds that this two-fold love of God and neighbor is "more than all whole burnt offerings and sacrifices" (Mark 12:32). Until this point there had been no mention of burnt offerings or sacrifice, yet it is completely on target. Jesus sees that he has answered wisely and says, "You are not far from the kingdom of God" (Mark 12:34). This scribe is close to the Kingdom of God precisely because he understands that God desires mercy and not sacrifice.

When we turn back to Luke, however, we find no mention of sacrifice by either the lawyer or Jesus. In place of the scribe's gloss on love over sacrifice, we find the parable. Although it is clearly about mercy, the parable makes no explicit mention of sacrifice. Still, can we read it as telling us something about the movement from sacrifice to mercy?

Here is the story:

A man was going down from Jerusalem to Jericho, and fell into the hands of robbers, who stripped him, beat him, and went away, leaving him half dead. ³¹Now by chance a priest was going down that road; and when he saw

him, he passed by on the other side. ³²So likewise a Levite, when he came to
the place and saw him, passed by on the other side. ³³But a Samaritan while
traveling came near him; and when he saw him, he was moved with pity.
³⁴He went to him and bandaged his wounds, having poured oil and wine
on them. Then he put him on his own animal, brought him to an inn, and
took care of him. ³⁵The next day he took out two denarii, gave them to the
innkeeper, and said, "Take care of him; and when I come back, I will repay
you whatever more you spend."

Perhaps the place to start is to pay attention to the violence that begins
the story. So often this parable is read as if it were a homily with the message,
"Don't turn your back on those in trouble." Today there are so-called Good
Samaritan laws that make it a crime to pass by an accident without rendering
aid, and that indemnify one from lawsuits should the aid be unsuccessful.
The man in the story, however, did not have an accident. He was set upon by
robbers, stripped, and beaten. He lay as if dead on the side of the road.

The story may seem anti-clerical. Not one but two priests pass by the
man. Both behave in the same way. They see the man beaten by robbers and
move to the other side of the road to avoid him, actually putting distance
between themselves and the victim. Why? Are we to conclude that they are
simply hard-hearted or perhaps that being a priest somehow makes one less
open to the suffering of others? The Greek word used to describe the beaten
man implies that he appears to be dead. The two priests, in other words,
see what appears to be a corpse lying on the side of the road. For a priest to
come into contact with a corpse would render him ritually impure and, thus,
unable to offer sacrifice. These are good priests who do what their religion
tells them they ought to do—keep away from a source of impurity.

Allow me to interrupt for a moment our focus on the scriptural text to
point out that these two priests are able to do what Leontius could not. The
religious sanction against impurity plays the role that anger is to play in the
Platonic system. It supports the "rational" part of the soul so that a person
can walk by the corpses without looking.

The Samaritan, the foreigner or "outsider," is moved by pity and "went to
him," as the Gospel so beautifully puts it. He moves in the opposite direction
from the priests. He bandages the victim's wounds, pouring oil and wine on
them. Oil and wine are things that could be used as offerings in sacrifice. Luke

is dramatizing here what the scribe in Mark's Gospel only stated: love is greater than any burnt offering or sacrifice. The elements of sacrifice are being applied to the broken body of the victim of violence. The detail suggests that the very energies that motivate sacrifice are now to be redirected toward the victim.

Having completed the parable, Jesus then poses a question to the lawyer: "Which of these three, do you think, was neighbor to the man who fell into the hands of the robbers?" (Luke 10:36). The lawyer's words are not without significance for those of us who are relearning how to read: "The one who showed him mercy." Jesus replies, "Go and do likewise." In fact, a more literal translation would be, "The one who *did* him mercy. Go and *do* likewise." Literally, that is, imitate the Samaritan.

The story of the Good Samaritan is thus about the love of neighbor, and it is one about how the traditional demands of religion, the demands for purity and sacrifice, can block that love. But there is always "more" to the story, just as love is always "more" than sacrifice. One way we unlock that "more" is to recall our own beginning. We want to find in ourselves those things that offend or scandalize us, so that we can hear our Lord say to us: "Go and learn the meaning of these words, 'I desire mercy, not sacrifice.'"

Although it may not be immediately apparent that the Parable of the Good Samaritan has anything to do with sacrifice, most people know that it was intended to offend. It has been given the title "Parable to the Good Samaritan," the implication being that all other Samaritans were not considered good. A gloss in John's Gospel tells us that Jews do not share things in common with Samaritans (John 4:9). The fact that this Samaritan does better than two Jewish priests can only be further grounds for offense.

While Jews listening to Jesus might have been offended by his portraying a Samaritan as the parable's hero, we tend to get more offended by the callousness of the priests who walk on by. Even when we understand that their motivation was religious and so not simply selfishness, we still can be offended that someone would let his religious practices interfere with at least determining whether someone is in need of help.

We can imagine other ways in which hearers or readers could be offended. For example, one who is not offended by priests might take offense with Jesus or with the Evangelist who are clearly presenting a distorted picture of the Jewish religion, a religion in which aiding someone in distress always overrides the Law. Our sensibilities may be less offended by someone's breaking a religious taboo than by someone's neglecting to help a fellow human being, but we can imagine people of a more traditional culture whose hierarchy of values is the reverse of our own. These people might be edified by the two priests who remain true to their religious beliefs, and offended that others can so easily override them. Perhaps these same people would not even be offended by that fact, and instead only find it realistic. The "other" doesn't know any better; he is only a Samaritan.

So, clearly there are various ways in which one could be offended by the story. As a matter of fact, we are not bound by religious taboos in the same way as first-century Jewish priests were or the way most of humanity has been since then. The reasons for this loosening of taboos are complex and hinted at by words such as "secularization" or "scientific progress." It has nothing to do with any supposed moral superiority on our part. In fact, the real danger would be to believe naively that for us, unlike the Jewish priests in the parable, there are no such things as the 'pure' and the 'impure,' that there is no in-group and out-group, no acceptable versus unacceptable. Any interpretation in which we know who the good guys and who the bad guys are weakens the story's import. Such distinctions simply reinforce our blindness to the subtle ways in which we have structured our world into an order that gives recognition to some and withholds it from others.

If we are, in fact, less likely to avoid a corpse because we no longer see it as a source of ritual impurity or, to use more current examples, if it is more difficult for one to be an overt anti-Semite in Germany or an overt racist in America today than it was seventy years ago, we should applaud that fact. That should not blind us, however, to the reality that the more obvious forms of bigotry have often been replaced by subtler ones that remain damaging to those excluded yet are essential for our identity as it is currently constructed.[11] We do exclude people. We have our criteria for judging whom we are merciful toward and whom we sacrifice. Again, any interpretation of the Jewish-Christian Scriptures that simply endorses our present style of life is bound to miss the mark.

The challenge to our present lifestyle that a scandalized reaction can represent is too interwoven into the parable for it to be anything other than essential. Thus, being able to be offended is a constitutive part of the consciousness of the person who hopes to move from sacrifice to mercy. Not to be scandalized can mean that we have reached the heights of holiness, but it can also mean that we have become so inured to the world that we have rendered ourselves incapable of being scandalized. We may think that we don't need scandal. Just accept everybody; live and let live. The significance of the obstacle that scandal represents to our accepted way of thinking is that our accepted way of thinking is not without its problems. Scandal is an essential aspect of religious consciousness. It is not simply negative. The victim who offends us also helps us to recognize that the "normal" way we do things is fundamentally flawed. So are we willing to let ourselves be scandalized in a way that challenges us? If being scandalized means letting ourselves be challenged and questioned by the victim, by the one whom we expelled or are about to expel, then living with, learning from, and overcoming scandal turns out to be the central issue of our religious lives.

One of the things that the Parable of the Good Samaritan teaches us is the difficulty of *not* predicating one's identity on the exclusion of the other. The Jewish priests' lives were centered on a God who demands sacrifice, and part and parcel of that demand was the demand for ritual purity and the exclusion of all who threatened to compromise it. The "sacrificial order"— that is, the religious and cultural order built upon the keeping of prohibitions and the offering of sacrifices—ensured the identity and security of most groups throughout human history. It is not enough, then, to make a conscious decision that I will no longer order my life by the exclusion of others. The consciousness making this decision is one formed by this very exclusion. The person who makes this kind of resolution is one short step away from excluding those who exclude others. If the Jewish priests in the parable ultimately failed in their religious duty by passing by the victim, so too have we failed when we condemn the priests for failing. Here, though, is a most perplexing point: if we do not condemn them, are we not condemned to condoning truly reprehensible behavior?

This way of reading the Parable of the Good Samaritan clarifies a central aspect of the admonition we have chosen as a guiding thread: "Go and learn the meaning of these words, 'I desire mercy, not sacrifice.'" The traditional religion of sacrifice is not just one option with mercy being another. The burnt offerings and sacrifices, the priesthood, the rituals and worship are not merely less important than the love of God and neighbor, but all of these things can form a block to the most essential expression of that love—showing mercy to the victim.

The solution is not to get rid of ritual and worship but rather to recognize that, just as the Jewish priests' religious sensibilities were offended by the presence of a seeming corpse, so the listeners outside the story are offended by Jesus' making the Samaritan the hero or by the priests' behavior. These stumbling blocks of offense, in a way analogous to the ritual and worship represented by the priests, are intended to be transformed into bridges to the deeper meaning of the mystery of Christ. Earlier we wondered where Jesus was directing us when he told the Pharisees to "Go and learn." When we heed this command and go to the Scriptures to learn the meaning of the words, what we find there are stumbling blocks, occasions for offense that seem to block our way and prevent us from going on. But these blocks are essential to the Gospel, essential to the way that we are to go. The stumbling blocks become bridges to understanding what we seek because they prevent us from accepting the meaning that is most convenient.

Let us assume that the lawyer who first asked the question that triggered the Parable of the Good Samaritan was offended that Jesus made the Samaritan more virtuous than the priests. Perhaps this is why, when Jesus asks him at the end of the parable who had been a neighbor to the man beaten by the robbers, the lawyer does not simply say "the Samaritan." Perhaps he cannot bring himself to use the word. Instead he says "the one who showed him mercy." Jesus then comments, "Go and do likewise."[12]

We do not know what became of the lawyer, but we are free to imagine that the story stayed with him. We also can imagine that he wondered over the words, "Go and do likewise." How many people lying half-dead on the side of the road was he likely to encounter? Perhaps, though, his reflections took another turn, and he recalled not the question that Jesus put to him about who was the neighbor in the parable, but rather his own question—"Who is my neighbor?"—an attempt to justify himself. The parable was originally a response to that question. Perhaps he went through the story again seeking the answer to *his* question. The answer is right on the surface. His neighbor is the one who comes to him when he is stripped, beaten, and left for dead.

In the tradition of the Church Fathers, the Christian faith would understand the human condition to be analogous to the position of the man lying beside the road. We are virtually dead and lying face-down in a ditch. We are corpses. Again, in the tradition of the Church Fathers, this reading allows one to identify Jesus with the figure of the Good Samaritan. Jesus is the one who comes to us and is merciful. Interpreting the parable in this way allows us to understand that first Jesus comes to us in our condition and shows us mercy; then we are enabled by this encounter to be merciful to others.

There is one more character in the story whose spiritual state we need to examine: the man who fell into the hands of the robbers. We can use our imaginations to see the man lying semi-conscious in the ditch and, at the same time, watching from a bird's-eye view what is happening to him. It is easy to think that he too will be offended at the behavior of the two priests as they pass by. 'I am not a corpse; I am a human being who needs your help,' he silently screams. But what about when the Samaritan comes, this one with whom "the Jews share nothing in common." He watches as the Samaritan approaches, begins to touch him, loosens his garments to apply wine and oil to his wounds. Is the man offended? Here the question is moot. In these kinds of situations we are simply grateful.

We need to keep this in mind as we explore further the implications of this story in Luke's Gospel. We are still being asked the central question: "How do you read?" Most of the time we are not aware that we are in the condition of the man lying in the ditch on the side of the road. Most of the time we make great efforts to prevent anything from reminding us of that condition, but the story indicates that this is where Christ will come to us. How can we come to occupy that place willingly?

Much commends this particular reading of the parable. It changes the parable from being a kind of moralistic story, one that leaves us with the feeling that we should be more considerate to those in need, into a parable that reveals how God works in our lives so that we might work in the lives of others. Relatively few persons come across the victim of violence in their actual experience, yet the parable cannot be directed only at them. It has a universal meaning that is about our salvation. The problem, though, with this interpretation is that, unlike the usual one that at least leaves us with a disturbed conscience, my interpretation can lead the reader to wait for God to show some mercy. There is no need for me to change until I am sure that I have had that experience. If each of us is the man lying beside the road, then each of us can wait for our good Samaritan to come.

The corrective is to remember that, whatever figurative interpretation we might give the story in order to let it speak to us, we always have to go back to the literal level. According to that level, the true victim is the target of actual violence. The figurative reading is valid only so long as it stays grounded in the literal meaning, and the victim of real violence is to be the literal object of our "mercy" right now. There should be no doubt about where our priorities lie—namely, with the victim of violence. With this background we are ready to explore the connection between religious life in the present age as consisting in our relationship to the victim of violence and religious life in its usual understanding as a set of rituals and dogmas.

Clearly, according to the position I have outlined here, the immediate criterion for whether anything is essentially religious would be the degree to which it brings us into solidarity with the victim. Just as clearly, my reading of the Good Samaritan story indicates that traditional religion—burnt offerings and sacrifices, the priesthood, rituals and worship—is not merely less important than the love of God and neighbor but can even form a block to the most essential expression of that love in showing mercy to the victim. This block that religion builds is the obstacle of scandal. The priests are scandalized by the presence of a corpse; we are scandalized at the behavior of the priests, or we are scandalized at the parable for making the priests look bad. Any one of these scandals, these obstacles, can become a bridge to the deeper reality of the victim. I believe that the purpose of the dogmas and rituals of the Christian faith is to keep us capable of experiencing and living with scandal.

Precisely here our attitude toward dogma has something to say to us at the beginning of the twenty-first century. We are no longer scandalized by a particular dogma. We are not going to war over the consubstantial nature of the Son with the Father. In the present it is instead dogma itself that seems offensive. No one is to be dogmatic. We often hear people saying that the various religions should forget their own doctrines and instead concentrate on the values that unite them with all other religions and people of good will. This outlook sounds promising, but it overlooks the role that scandal plays in our salvation. Even if it is not Christian scandal, the idea that rational thought is inadequate for dealing with the mystery of life is a commonplace among religions, as is the idea that our normal way of operating is enmeshed in illusion. One way in which our normal way of operating gets exposed for what it truly is occurs through dogma and ritual.

One can say with complete justification that dogmas are rational attempts to understand certain mysteries of the faith. I would point out, however, that, when Christianity defines such things as the Trinity as being a mystery *in senso strictum*, this means that it is beyond rational comprehension. It is worthwhile to attempt to understand the mystery as best we can, but it seems to me that dogma functions here in a negative way by telling us when we have gone wrong. And the ultimate reason is that our misunderstanding will rob the mystery of its mystery and thereby of its scandal. The scandal of dogma protects the scandal of faith.

The sacraments of the Christian Church are the very stuff of religious scandal. The scandalous nature of proclaiming a piece of bread to be the flesh of Christ and a cup of wine to be his blood should not be overlooked due to familiarity. The sense of scandal in the sacraments is to open our eyes to the mystery of reality. It can be a scandal to realize that everyday things are bearers of the Godhead. God is no longer safely up in His heaven. The quotidian struggle of ordinary human beings is suffused with grace and marred by sin. Grace emerges in this violent world like a man moved by pity at the sight of someone lying on the edge of the road, like salvation through a man on the Cross.

The work of parables, dogma, and sacraments is the work of Christ himself. It is a gateway to salvation but one that can only be approached via the constantly annulled possibility of scandal. Thus, if we do not suffer the temptation to be scandalized, if we are not tempted, every now and again, to throw the Bible across the room because of its offense, we are probably missing something. Only when parable, dogma, and ritual are blocks to our understanding can they be bridges to deeper understanding. This is so because the natural man is heading toward death and sees life only as being the opposite of death, when in fact true life does not stand over against death but encompasses, includes, transforms, and transfigures it.

We can now return to our story, concerning which a final question confronts us. How does one get the vision of the Samaritan without condemning the vision of the priests? How does one become the kind of person whose religious sensibilities move him toward rather than away from the victim?

The Gospel gives us some clues. The Parable of the Good Samaritan is part one of a two-part story. The second is the story of Martha and Mary. Although not a parable, it has been treated like one since the times of the Church Fathers. That is, the Church has regarded Martha and Mary as allegorical figures for different states in the Christian life, most notably the active life and the contemplative life respectively.

Scholars have pointed out how Luke ties these two stories together. Beyond the simple juxtaposition, one hidden by the subtitles and paragraph breaks that modern editions insert, we notice that the first story opens with the words "A man was going down." There is nothing unusual here, but the next section opens with the words "A certain woman by the name of Martha." It is an odd construction and seems to be there only for the purpose of making it grammatically parallel with the opening of the Good Samaritan story. The parallel is strengthened by the fact that the first story features a man as its main character and the second story a woman. Luke often employs a doublet in which two stories or sayings alternate between featuring a man and a woman, the most obvious example being first Zecharias and the announcement of the birth of John and then Mary and the announcement of the birth of Jesus.[13]

Here is the story:

> [38]Now as they went on their way, he entered a certain village, where a woman named Martha welcomed him into her home. [39]She had a sister named Mary, who sat at the Lord's feet and listened to what he was saying. [40]But Martha was distracted by her many tasks; so she came to him and asked, "Lord, do you not care that my sister has left me to do all the work by myself? Tell her then to help me." [41]But the Lord answered her, "Martha, Martha, you are worried and distracted by many things; [42]there is need of only one thing. Mary has chosen the better part, which will not be taken away from her."

Rather than look at this story as being complementary to the Parable of the Good Samaritan in that the first emphasizes love of neighbor while the second emphasizes love of God, I want to focus on the complementary figures of the man on the one hand and of Martha and Mary on the other. The man beaten by robbers is the victim to whom mercy is extended. The grace of God comes to him in a way that he did not choose and under other circumstances might not have been able to accept. In contrast, Jesus comes to Martha and Mary in their home. Unlike the man, Martha is in a position to welcome him and does so. Still, his coming is not without its problems for her. Martha is offended that her sister does not help her, and she is further offended that the Lord does not seem to care about this lack of help. The immediate meaning of this second story is that Jesus does *not* come to the aid of Martha and, in fact, refuses to do so.

Jesus is the neighbor or Samaritan in this story, and "neighbor" in the Gospel now has a soteriological function—a saving function. When Jesus says to the lawyer at the end of the Good Samaritan story, "Go and do likewise," it is either a seemingly impossible command or a revelation that Jesus' mercy toward us will bear fruit in our being merciful to others. He is not saying in simplistic fashion 'Go and be nice to people.' He is not saying 'Go and help people complete the various projects by which they build up their identity, like the one in which Martha is engaged.' Instead, he is saying something much more radical and demanding. He says in effect, 'Go and be an occasion of salvation in people's lives. Be a bringer of grace, peace, and life.'

In spite of the illustrious heritage of the interpretation that views Martha and Mary as representing the active and contemplative life, one can also see them as representing two ways of reading the Gospel or two ways of listening to the Lord. On the one hand, we can read as those given to offense. This means that we read the Gospels as texts meant to help us accomplish what we are about. Like Martha, we demand from the Lord that he order the world to conform to our wishes. Upset with Christ that he does not meet our expectations, that he does not help us with our projects, and that he does not command others to do so the same, we complain about our heavy burdens that no one, except we ourselves, has asked us to bear.

On the other hand, we can read the Gospels as those not given to offense. The figure of Mary harks back to the scribe in Mark's Gospel who says, in effect, that love is much "more" than offerings or sacrifices. This "more," this "better," is what Mary chooses. Without distorting the meaning too much, we can see Martha's service as a "sacrifice of service." It is a noble and good thing, but God desires something more. He desires mercy; He desires love. To love God and our neighbor is to choose what is "better." It is to sit "at the Lord's feet."

Luke delicately suggests a parallel not only between Martha and the man beaten by robbers but also between Mary and him. Mary is not a victim of violence, but she freely chooses what he is forced to accept—that which is better. For him it is mercy at the hands of a Samaritan; for Mary it is to sit at the feet of Jesus. The reception of this mercy caused offense in others: the lawyer is offended at the thought of a "good Samaritan," Martha is offended that the Lord does not tell Mary to help her, and, probably, we as readers are offended. Still, Jesus tells the parable to the lawyer; he answers Martha's objections; he gives us these Scriptures. Our being offended does not offend him, rather he offers these opportunities to be scandalized precisely so that we can overcome our scandal and enter more deeply into the mystery. His words to Martha can be read as an invitation to imitate Mary.

So there is, finally, a third position from which we can read. We can identify with the man who fell into the hands of robbers, lying half-dead in a ditch and having been abandoned by those from whom one might most expect to receive help. In that case we probably do not need to read. The words of Scripture will come to us, unbidden, in all their terrible beauty. They will come to us like wine and oil poured onto wounds—excruciating in pain, soothing in comfort, but healing in effect.

I want to take all that we have learned from the Parable of the Good Samaritan as well as from the story of Martha and Mary and, without reducing it to a formula or principle, maintain that it is an answer to Jesus' question, "How do you read?" We read like Mary, sitting at the feet of the Lord; we read like Martha, distracted by many things; we read like the lawyer, trying to justify ourselves; we read like the priests, vindicating ourselves in walking by; we read like the benevolent Samaritan, seeing a victim of violence; we read like the man who fell into the hands of robbers, from the perspective of the victim. All of these stances represent an answer to the question, "How do you read?" but they do not produce equally valid readings. Only some of them open our eyes to the importunate truth of victimization.

CHAPTER 6

The Challenge of Flannery O'Connor

The Scandal of Flannery O'Connor

We began this journey with Leontius's encounter with the corpses. We saw there that we both want and do not want to encounter reality at its deepest level. We long for it and dread it at the same time. We then widened our perspective through some reflections on language. Words, spelled out in her palm, opened up a glorious world for Helen Keller as a child. These same words, though, can also close off reality, rendering it nugatory. Neither the opportunity nor the danger can be avoided. Even a glance, held a moment too long, may bring the kind of encounter with reality that demands to be named. Philosophy, literature, theology, and the Scriptures can give us that name—that is, they can help to articulate the reality we are experiencing. But they also can become a block to that reality. Standing before the grave of Lazarus, Jesus tells Martha that her brother will rise again. Martha responds with a "textbook-perfect" formula of faith: "I know that he will rise again in the resurrection on the last day" (Jn. 11:24). In spite of its literal perfection, it does not satisfy Jesus but calls forth something more. The true words Martha has spoken have to become rooted in the person of Christ to reveal their true meaning: "I am the resurrection and the life" (Jn. 11:25). The stumbling block, the stone, has to be removed. With the stone's removal, with Lazarus's resurrection the reality of Jesus' life and death is revealed.

This pattern where the "place" of misunderstanding or non-understanding gets transformed to the "place" of deeper understanding is familiar to literary theorists. Many of them suggest that in mediating the encounter between her reader and reality, an author will be forced to use all of her craft not only to present the real but also to overcome the reader's built-in defenses against the encounter. The place of most resistance can, with skill and luck, become the place of deepest insight. This is often expressed by saying that the author has to create not only the work but also the reader.

I think that this is especially true of Flannery O'Connor because she understood how much she had to overcome to get her vision across. In one of her famous critical statements about her own fiction, O'Connor wrote: "When you can assume that your audience holds the same beliefs as you do, you can relax a little and use more normal means of talking to it; when you have to assume that it does not, then you have to make your vision apparent by shock—to the hard of hearing you shout, and for the almost-blind, you draw large and startling figures."[1] This sentiment helps to explain not only her use of the grotesque but also her deliberate use of scandal.

Her short stories and novels deliver a salutary shock in the kind of prose that leaves one asking for more. This shock is not just that of an unexpected turn of events, nor do her stories have the uncanny quality of the corpses that Leontius both longed to look at yet dreaded to see. Instead, her work attracts the reader through its beauty, which gets manifested in and through some pretty gritty reality. A part of the beauty, I might add, is her humor, which is not gallows humor but laughter earned through the challenge to serious thought.

All of this is a way of saying that one path for us to become more familiar with the way that scandal, as an obstacle to understanding, can become a bridge to deeper understanding is to look at the art of Flannery O'Connor. We need to exercise a certain amount of caution here. I do not believe that O'Connor's ultimate goal in her stories was to cause scandal; we know from her correspondence that she struggled with this question.[2] O'Connor was keenly aware that her intention not to cause scandal was not enough to prevent it from happening. "What leads the writer to his salvation [looking at the worst in the world as an exercise of trust in God] may lead the reader into sin," she wrote, "and the Catholic writer who looks at this possibility directly looks the Medusa in the face and is turned to stone" (*CW*, 810). Dante, we recall, faced a similar moment in his writing of the *Divine Comedy*. To name reality justly is to run the risk of spiritual petrification. The best and worst possibilities co-exist, side by side.

O'Connor saw her task as a writer in terms that she borrowed from Joseph Conrad: "'to render the highest justice possible to the visible universe.'" She hopes, again quoting Conrad, "'by the power of the written word, to make you [the reader] hear, to make you feel . . . , before all, to make you *see.*'"[3] She portrays reality but, contrary to what one might expect, does not see art as making the reader see *what she sees.* Writing is not, in her words, a "missionary activity."[4] Because she has great faith in reality's capacity to speak to each individual, she does not feel a need to impose her vision on the reader. Instead, she dramatizes reality so that the reader may apprehend it.[5]

O'Connor dramatizes reality in such a way that allows the reader to see beneath its surface. This kind of penetrating vision is accomplished through the unification of reason and imagination. To be reasonable for her means "to find, in the object, in the situation, in the sequence, the spirit which makes it itself."[6] And this is "only done by the violence of a single-minded respect for the truth."[7]

For O'Connor this violence, this single-minded respect for the truth, is at the heart of her art. The violence here is obviously not directed against the truth, but neither is it directed against the other. It can only be directed against herself. It is a violence against the barriers in herself that prevent her from reaching the truth. We might go so far as to say that with O'Connor this is violence against scandal, scandal being the obstacle to truth. O'Connor experiences an internal imperative to overcome the obstacles that block her way to the truth. The scandal, which the reader can experience in reading her fiction, can be triggered by the various violent acts represented in her texts, but most often it is a reaction to the juxtaposition of that violence with grace. Some readers, confronted with her violent overcoming of scandal, can see only the violence and not what is being overcome.

For O'Connor, then, violence has its uses. She was aware of complaints against the prevalence of violence in modern fiction, where it is assumed that "this violence is a bad thing and meant to be an end in itself."[8] Violence, for

O'Connor, is never an end in itself. It is always accompanied by a manifestation of grace. She writes:

> In my own stories I have found that violence is strangely capable of returning my characters to reality and preparing them to accept their moment of grace. Their heads are so hard that almost nothing else will do the work. This idea, that reality is something to which we must be returned at considerable cost, is one which is seldom understood by the casual reader, but it is one which is implicit in the Christian view of the world.[9]

By presenting her protagonists' struggle of being returned to reality, O'Connor hopes to effect her reader's analogous return to reality, and toward that end she uses a certain amount of violence. So we have the violence that O'Connor practiced against her own scandal at the truth, the violence that gets represented in the text, and finally the violence that she hopes the reader will now exercise against his or her own scandal at the truth. Can we specify these levels of violence and perhaps indicate the grace for which O'Connor also hoped?

At the most fundamental level in terms of her experience as an author— that is, beyond any scandal that the reader might experience and any scandal that might be represented in the stories—there is Flannery O'Connor's own feelings about her novels. By way of contrast, she displays no such sense of scandal regarding her short stories. Obviously her scandal didn't stem from shock at what she had written. There was, however, a scandalous element in the way she regarded her two novels. She said she hated writing them yet her correspondence indicates that she also lived for them. She dedicated years to them, and these years were oftentimes of great struggle. Her short stories, on the other hand, seemed to come almost naturally to her. They were often described as a relief or an escape from the particular novel on which she was working. And while she could read her own short stories and laugh until she remembered with a little embarrassment that she had written them, she had a difficult time reading the page proofs of her second novel, *The Violent Bear It Away*. She writes in a letter at the time, "The proofs came early and seeing the thing in print very nearly made me sick. It all seemed awful to me. There seemed too much to correct to make correcting anything feasible" (*CW*, 1108–9). It is also important to note, lest I give a one-sided view here, that O'Connor was also able to write: "Everything in it [*The Violent Bear It Away*] seems to me to be inevitable in the economy of the situation." On some level she knew she had overcome the obstacles.

We will look in more detail at the precise nature of the scandal O'Connor faced in *The Violent Bear It Away*, but first I want to turn to Girard for help in deepening our understanding of both the obstacle to the truth and the nature of the violence required to overcome that obstacle. The primary obstacle to truth is violence itself, and so violence can become the primary bridge to truth. To overcome this violence violently is, at the very least, paradoxical and may well be contradictory. Before jumping to that conclusion, however, we need to take a step back and begin by understanding the obstacles to understanding that the obstacle to truth is violence. The difficulty of that sentence lies not so much in its grammatical construction as in our own resistance to this fundamental truth. If we do not begin here, there is a danger that we will remain in the land of misunderstanding, thinking that we are seeing when in fact we are blind.

The difficulty begins not with violence, which is often obvious, but with our own desires. Returning once again to the image from Plato, the corpses are obvious, although many readers reduce them to a status analogous to that of the casualties of an accident rather than acknowledging them as the victims of state-sponsored violence. What is problematic is desire. Leontius wants to look, and he wants to turn away. He is drawn toward the corpses, and he is repelled. He is, in a word, fascinated.

To understand the way these desires, spawned by violence, can prevent us from grasping the truth that violence itself prevents us from seeing the truth of violence, I turn again to *Deceit, Desire, and the Novel.* There Girard exposes the paradox that novelists "reveal the truth of desire in their great novels. But this truth remains hidden even at the heart of the revelation. The reader, who is usually convinced of his own spontaneity, applies to the work the meanings he already applies to the world" (16). In other words, the reader believes a lie, one that both is rooted in and brings forth violence. This lie is the meaning that the reader applies both to the world and to the text.

The great novelist is aware not only of the truth but also of the lie. She is aware of the lie first in herself and also in the reader. The lie can seem innocent enough: I want what I want because I want it; my desires are mine and arise from myself alone. But this is a deceptive view not only of oneself but also of the world, and, as Girard says, it then gets applied to otherwise revelatory texts in such a way that the texts themselves seem to add their weight to the lie. The romantic reading of Cervantes's *Don Quixote* is one example that Girard gives.

We have already seen the way that this lie leads to violence. We recall here that the violence that results from the romantic lie transcends not just the individuals who make up the community but also the community itself, since this violence organizes that community as a social body. It can be difficult to distinguish the kind of transcendence based on violence from true transcendence based on love. Girard tells us that "to rid ourselves of this confusion, to detect transcendent love—which remains invisible beyond the transcendent violence that stands between—we have to accept the idea that human violence is a deceptive worldview and recognize how the forms of misunderstanding that arise from it operate" (*TH*, 217). Much like the similarities between the romantic lie of spontaneous desire and the novelistic truth of mimetic desire described in *Deceit, Desire, and the Novel*, the two forms of transcendence appear to be almost identical. Further, the analogies between the two forms of transcendence transcend any cultural differences so that, from a cultural viewpoint, they amount to very much the same thing. This makes possible "almost instantaneous conversion" between them in spite of there being also a "radical, an abysmal opposition" (*TH*, 217).

In order to understand both the similarities and differences of these two forms of transcendence, let us read Girard's description of the impossibility of the truth about violence being revealed to a human being caught up in a violent situation. We do not have in our own power, he argues, the language for this kind of revelation.

> Either you are violently opposed to violence and inevitably play its game, or you are not opposed to it, and it shuts your mouth immediately. In other words, the regime of violence cannot possibly be brought out into the open. . . . This unprecedented task of revealing the truth about violence requires a man who is not obliged to violence for anything and does not think in terms of violence—someone who is capable of talking back to violence while remaining entirely untouched by it.
>
> It is impossible for such a human being to arise in a world completely ruled by violence and the myths based on violence. In order to understand

that you cannot see and make visible the truth except by taking the place of the victim, you must already be occupying that place; yet to take that place, you must already be occupying that place; yet to take that place, you must already be in possession of the truth. You cannot become aware of the truth unless you act in opposition to the laws of violence, and you cannot act in opposition to these laws unless you already grasp the truth. All mankind is caught within this vicious circle. For this reason the Gospels and the whole New Testament, together with the theologians of the first councils, proclaim that Christ is God not because he was crucified, but because he is God born of God from all eternity. (*TH* 218–19)

The violence that allows one to see the revelation is a violence that acts "in opposition to the laws of violence." Here we come up against the limits of language. On the one hand, if one is "violently opposed to violence," then one "inevitably play[s] its game." If one does not oppose it, it silences one immediately. So one has to act in opposition to its laws, and the only language we have for this kind of action is that of violence. Thus, while the laws of violence are a lie, O'Connor's "violence of a single-minded respect for truth" is one way we have for expressing the means by which human beings get to the reality of love. Perhaps here we have one of the most basic forms of scandal: willy-nilly we are involved in violence, even in our attempts to avoid it. O'Connor was not scandalized by this human situation; instead, she was able to "see and make visible the truth," and that means, according to Girard, that she somehow occupied the place of the victim.

O'Connor took the place of the victim through her "violence of a single-minded respect for truth," which means that the violence was directed against herself and that she found "in the object, in the situation, in the sequence, the spirit which makes it itself." She found, in other words, the spirit that makes the victim the victim. That is, she found the spirit of truth that makes every victim into an *alter Christus*, another Christ. This is in contrast to Rousseau who found a way to make himself into the only victim, into a sole *alter Christus*. Since O'Connor did this in her novels and short stories, it is to her fiction that we now must turn. There are some peculiar difficulties in writing about O'Connor's fiction for people who are not familiar with it. Let me take a moment to outline these challenges in order to make intelligible my way of treating her writings.

First of all, it is difficult to summarize an O'Connor story without its sounding ridiculous. The bare bones of the plot never succeed in transmitting the depth at which she operates. Second, it is not easy to analyze her fiction without giving away the shocking moments that she labored to make as effective as possible and that lose their effectiveness when removed from the narrative context. Finally, and as a consequence of these two reasons, I find that commenting directly on her fiction discourages some people from wanting to read her—the very opposite of the effect I would like to have. I therefore have chosen to emphasize some of her nonfiction and an incident from her second novel, knowledge of which will not spoil the experience of reading it for the first time.

O'Connor's vision, whether expressed in either her essays or fiction, is rooted in a belief, similar to Girard's, that the Gospel revelation contains the power of deconstructing culture. Her essays evince a high degree of conscious control over her art, and there is much that can be learned from them, but for our purposes the most enlightening reflections concerning the role of violence are contained in the only piece she wrote to introduce someone else's writing.

A Memoir of Mary Ann

Throughout the late 1950s until her untimely death in 1964 O'Connor was a successful writer living in rural Georgia who answered every letter addressed to her. Naturally, some of these letters came from people seeking her help in breaking into the publishing world or recommending different projects to which she might turn her authorial hand. One such letter came from a group of nuns in Atlanta who wanted O'Connor to write the biography of girl they had cared for and whom they considered to be a saint. O'Connor was aware that her gifts as a writer did not extend to making a child saint come alive. She could do much more with a child demon. She thus suggested to the sisters that it would be much better if they wrote the biography themselves and that, when they were finished, she would edit the manuscript. She wrote: "I felt that a few attempts to capture Mary Ann in writing would lead them to think better of the project. It was doubtful that any of them had the literary gifts of their foundress. Moreover, they were busy nurses and had their hands full following a strenuous vocation" (*CW*, 828). The manuscript O'Connor soon received was about a young girl who lived from the age of three until her death at twelve in a charity home in Atlanta run by a Dominican order called the Servants of Relief for Incurable Cancer. Mary Ann had been born with a tumor on the side of her face. Its removal involved the loss of one eye and the general distortion of her face. However, to quote a Sister, "after one meeting one was never conscious of her physical defect but recognized only the brave spirit and felt the joy of such contact" (*CW*, 822).

It so happens that this particular order of sisters was founded by Rose Hawthorne, the daughter of Nathaniel. O'Connor used this historical background to pluck out an episode from Hawthorne's *Our Old Home* for comment. In it, a certain fastidious gentleman, while going through a Liverpool workhouse, is followed by a poor, dirty child who manifests a desire to be held. The gentleman was English, shy of human contact, wary of dirt, and accustomed to detached observation. He hesitated and struggled. Hawthorne writes: "So I watched the struggle in his mind with a good deal of interest, and am seriously of the opinion that he did a heroic act and effected more than he dreamed of toward his final salvation when he took up the loathsome child and caressed it as tenderly as if he had been its father" (*CW*, qtd. 824–25). This episode in the novel is based, in fact, on an incident in Hawthorne's own life. Hawthorne's wife published his notebooks after his death, and they contain an account of the incident that differs in details but corresponds closely to its representation in the novel.

Hawthorne's daughter wrote that her father's words about the incident in the Liverpool workhouse were among the greatest he had ever written. For O'Connor their greatness is confirmed by the fruit they bore. She recognizes a relationship between the words of the father, the acts of the daughter, and the life of Mary Ann.

> She [Hawthorne's daughter] discovered much that he sought, and fulfilled in a practical way the hidden desires of his life. The ice in the blood which he feared, and which this very fear preserved him from, was turned by her into a warmth which initiated action. If he observed, fearfully but truthfully; if he acted, reluctantly but firmly, she charged ahead, secure in the path his truthfulness had outlined for her. (*CW*, 826)

This charging ahead by Rose Hawthorne led her to Catholicism, to founding an order of nuns, and to establishing homes to care for those with incurable cancer. Eventually it led to a group of women caring for Mary Ann and being so impressed with her life that they felt compelled to write an account for publication. Ultimately it resulted in the introduction that O'Connor wrote for the work. That piece allowed O'Connor to reflect on the culture in which she found herself, a culture that would ask not so much why Mary Ann had to die at such a tender age but why such a deformed person should be born in the first place.

O'Connor writes:

> One of the tendencies of our age is to use the suffering of children to discredit the goodness of God, and once you have discredited His goodness, you are done with Him. . . . Busy cutting down human imperfection, they are making headway also on the raw material of the good. Ivan Karamazov cannot believe, as long as one child is in torment; Camus' hero cannot accept the divinity of Christ, because of the massacre of the innocents. In this popular pity, we mark our gain in sensibility and our loss in vision. If other ages felt less, they saw more, even though they saw with the blind, prophetical, unsentimental eye of acceptance, which is to say, of faith. In the absence of this faith now, we govern by tenderness. It is a tenderness which, long since cut off from the person of Christ, is wrapped in theory. When tenderness is detached from the source of tenderness, its logical outcome is terror. It ends in the forced labor camps and in the fumes of the gas chamber. (*CW*, 830–31)

So O'Connor is aware of the logic of scandal. The authors to whom she refers are scandalized by the human condition, and they question the goodness of God. This logic begins for O'Connor with a separation of tenderness from Christ, the source of love, and it ends in the apocalypse.[10] She is aware also of another logic, "a direct line between the incident in the Liverpool work-house, the work of Hawthorne's daughter[,] and Mary Ann—who stands not only for herself but for all the other examples of human imperfection and grotesquerie which the Sisters of Rose Hawthorne's order spend their lives caring for" (*CW*, 831). In this quotation, between the incident in the workhouse and the work of Hawthorne's daughter, O'Connor leaves out the notebooks and novels of Nathaniel Hawthorne. She leaves out the role that literature plays in this "direct line," while emphasizing it in the other case by taking her examples from literature. I do not believe this accidental.

All great authors are keenly aware of the potential for evil in literature. Dante, for example, characterizes the book that Franscesco and Paulo were reading and that led to their fatal kiss as "Galeotto." Girard comments: "Galleot (or Galehalt) is the treacherous knight, Arthur's enemy, who sows the seeds of passion in the hearts of Lancelot and Guinevere. It is the book itself, Francesca maintains, that plays the role of the diabolical go-between, the pander, in her life."[11] For Cervantes the romances that Don Quixote read caused his insanity. The instances could be multiplied. Perhaps this literary connection is why O'Connor observes that these two lines are "not so far removed" from each other. In any case O'Connor is explicit about one thing: it is the *story* of Mary Ann that "will illuminate the lines that join the most diverse lives and that hold us fast in Christ" (*CW*, 831).

The story of Mary Ann, however, is not an O'Connor story, and it does not even provide the makings for one. She herself admits her inability to illuminate goodness. We turn, then, to O'Connor's fiction to find the other logic of scandal that goes from tenderness and pity to the gas chamber.

The Character of Rayber

In her second novel, *The Violent Bear It Away*, O'Connor has a character who uses the suffering of children to discredit the goodness of God. His name is Rayber Tarwater, and he is the nephew of a backwoods prophet, Mason; the uncle of the protagonist, Francis Tarwater (known simply as Tarwater); and father to a mentally disabled child named Bishop. Rayber had been kidnapped at the age of seven, taken to the farm, and baptized by Mason. He has grown up to become a school teacher and an empiricist of the most narrow kind.

Of all the characters in the novel the one whose age and educational background most resembles the novelist's is the one most estranged from her. O'Connor writes in her correspondence, "Anyway I am usually out of my depth, and I don't really know Rayber or have the ear for him" (*CW*, 1109). Of even more significance from our perspective is her observation that

"Rayber, of course, was always the stumbling block" (1109). He is her scandal. This was the character (along with Enoch in *Wise Blood*) who, O'Connor acknowledged, weakened the novel but also made it possible. "It is strange that in both these novels," she writes, "what makes them possible as novels, I mean what makes them work, is the same thing that detracts or lowers the interest. . . . I was five years on *WB* and seven on this one[;] . . . I spent most of the seven years on Rayber" (*CW*, 1109). This is analogous to my definition of scandal as an impossible necessity or necessary impossibility. The very thing that rendered O'Connor's writing seemingly impossible was necessary to the writing of the novel.

O'Connor struggled to make Rayber more than a caricature. Although she protested that "the old man"—that is, the old man Mason, the figure of the Old Testament prophet—"speaks for me," the novel was born of her own scandal at the recalcitrant figure of a believing disbeliever. In the end, O'Connor was able to assert, "Everything in it seems to be inevitable in the economy of the situation." It is the logic that underlies the inevitability that interests us here.

The figure of Rayber is important because he allows O'Connor to deal thematically not just with the clear-cut options of belief or unbelief but with the more complex reality of unbelief due to someone else's belief. That is, the character allows her the possibility of distinguishing true from false scandal. The Gospel's call and mission can cause scandal but in two very different ways. On the one hand, a person can fall away because the demands of the Gospel are too great. On the other hand, a person can fall away because of the way the message is presented. Rayber interprets his experience of his own call by as an instance of being scandalized by his uncle. From Rayber's viewpoint this experience was simply evil, but O'Connor's viewpoint is more complex. For her there is first true charity, then its perversion in seduction and scandal, and finally there is the false interpretation of true charity as its own perversion.

At the basis of Rayber's relationship with his uncle, the prophet, is the toxic mix of love and shame that constitutes scandal in its most personal form. Early in the novel O'Connor emphasizes this quality in their relationship: "And once, only once, the old man [Mason] had leaned forward and said to Tarwater, in a voice that could no longer contain the pleasure of its secret, 'He [Rayber] loved me like a daddy and he was ashamed of it!'" (*CW*,

375). Rayber himself admits that he is never completely free from the old man's influence. All that he can do is continually to fight it off.

This necessity of a constant struggle results in Rayber's life of asceticism. Girard tells us that "*Askesis* for the sake of desire is the inevitable consequence of triangular desire. It can therefore be found in the work of all the novelists of that desire."[12] It can be found there because, in order to reveal mimetic desire, one has to see through this false asceticism to its real source in rivalry and not in transcendent love. Thus, the asceticism is a manifestation of "deviated" transcendence, which requires great sacrifice, and Rayber is a true adherent. This kind of transcendence takes one beyond oneself but only as far as the rival. It ends in an interpersonal struggle for domination. Rayber struggles with his uncle, but he also ends up struggling against what his uncle represents: true transcendence.

> He had kept it [the transcendent love that afflicts his uncle and Tarwater] from gaining control over him by what amounted to a rigid ascetic discipline. He did not look at anything too long, he denied his senses unnecessary satisfactions. He slept in a narrow iron bed, worked sitting in a straight-backed chair, ate frugally, spoke little, and cultivated the dullest for friends. . . . He was not deceived that this was a whole or a full life, he only knew that it was the way his life had to be lived if it were going to have any dignity at all. (*CW*, 402)

For Rayber, even though this is not a full life, he does recognize that "in silent ways he lived an heroic life" (*CW*, 402).

His chance at a full life was "ruined" by his uncle because, as Rayber explains it to Mason, "A child can't defend himself. Children are cursed with believing. You pushed me out of the real world and I stayed out of it, until I didn't know which was which. You infected me with your idiot hopes, your foolish violence" (*CW*, 376–77). For O'Connor the uncle's hopes were not idiotic, and his violence may have been foolish but only in the sense that God's wisdom is foolishness to us. This is perhaps an example of the price for being restored to reality, and that price in fiction can be represented as violence.

O'Connor is showing something more, however. Through her art she makes concrete the way divine realities can be read or understood in two diametrically opposed ways. Rayber accuses his uncle of the most serious sin in the New Testament—scandalizing "little ones." In Matthew's Gospel Jesus says, "But if any of you put a stumbling block before one of these little ones who believe in me it would be better for you if a great millstone were fastened around your neck and you were drowned in the depth of the sea" (Matt. 18:6). O'Connor is raising the question of whether telling a young person of his adoption by God, brotherhood in Christ, and spiritual vocation is to scandalize the child. Rayber certainly feels victimized. As we shall see, O'Connor's answer is not unambiguous.

The episode on which I wish to focus has Rayber standing outside an evangelical Protestant mission in the dead of night. He has been following his nephew who snuck out one night, and this is where he ends up tracking him. Looking through a small window that gives him a side view of the stage, the first words he hears are "Suffer the little children to come unto Him." These words are spoken as a way of introduction for a twelve-year-old girl to prophesy. All Rayber can hear in that sentence, however, is violent exploitation: "Another child exploited, Rayber thought furiously. It was the thought of a child's mind warped, of a child led away from reality that always enraged him, bringing back to him his own childhood's seduction" (*CW*, 408). Rayber is clearly scandalized. In fact, the sight of the child prophet infuriates Rayber. His "fury encompassed the parents, the preacher, all the idiots he could not see who were sitting in front of the child, parties to her degradation" (*CW*, 411–12). The yield of Rayber's scandal at this spectacle is pity or a kind of tenderness: "His pity encompassed all exploited children—himself when he was child, Tarwater exploited by the old man, this child exploited by parents, Bishop exploited by the very fact that he was alive" (*CW*, 412). The fury and the pity balance one another. They allow Rayber to divide the world between the exploiters he rages against and the exploited whom he pities.

Over against both Rayber's fury and his pity O'Connor contrasts love by having the little girl embody the "blind, prophetical, unsentimental eye" of faith. It is with that eye that she sees Rayber's face in the window and sees his pity while she speaks to the crowd inside of love. It is a love that knows no pity, that "cuts like the cold wind" (*CW*, 413).

According to the girl, the world has its hopes, and these hopes are not just different from those of believers but diametrically opposed to them.

The world hopes what any of us would hope if it were our child who was in danger of being killed because some lunatic in authority, like Herod in Matthew's Gospel, was searching for a child in order to kill him. We would hope, if worst came to worst, that he would find the child who is *not* our child. The little girl in O'Connor's novel says, "The world hoped old Herod would slay the right child, the world hoped old Herod wouldn't waste those children but he wasted them. He didn't get the right one. Jesus grew up and raised the dead" (*CW*, 413). The world's hope was disappointed; Christian hope was not. Jesus grew up and raised the dead. The death of the Holy Innocents then took on a much larger meaning. It became a part of a counter-narrative opposing violence. What O'Connor saw with piercing clarity is that to hope out of a tenderness divorced from Christ that the Holy Innocents had been spared is to hope against salvation. It is to grant those innocents a longer life on earth at the cost of denying them eternal life. It is to accept death as having the last word.

Rayber thus responds to the girl's profession of faith that Jesus raised the dead by denying it. According to him, Jesus did not raise the Holy Innocents from the dead. All the children to whom Rayber's pity has been extended have been left not just bereft by Jesus but seduced in his name into a realm of non-being. Over against the girl's vision of Jesus' Second Coming, Rayber has "a vision of himself moving like an avenging angel through the world, gathering up all the children that the Lord, not Herod, had slain" (*CW*, 413). With these words O'Connor crystallizes the Girardian *misrecognition* that lies at the heart of Rayber's scandal at Jesus. He attributes the violence of the slaughter of the innocents to Jesus rather than to Herod. O'Connor sees his response as the world's reaction to the violent entry of grace into its midst.

The Rayber who moves "like an avenging angel through the world" is in rivalry with Jesus (*CW*, 413). He wants to save, he wants to gather, he wants to protect and teach, not with Jesus and as part of his mission but against Jesus and on his own. He is a demonic parody of Jesus, a scandalized version of him. "Come away with me! . . . I'll save you, beautiful child!" he silently implores, but the child continues to speak of a Word of God that burns clear. "Her eyes," we read, "were large and dark and fierce." Rayber feels that "in the space between them, their spirits had broken the bonds of age and ignorance and were mingling in some unheard of knowledge of each other. . . . Suddenly she raised her arm and pointed toward his face: 'I see a damned soul before my eye! I see a dead man Jesus hasn't raised'" (*CW*, 414–15). Rayber's head drops from the window "as if it had been struck by an invisible bolt." This is a moment of grace for him, but he experiences it as a moment of violence. When he finally gets away from her shrieking voice, "a silent dark relief enclosed him like shelter after a tormenting wind" (*CW*, 415). The relief is dark because it is not from God. The tormenting wind is the Holy Spirit, but Rayber refuses to recognize it.

O'Connor's novel thus would seem quite clear: Rayber is the opposite of those who are blest because they find no scandal in Jesus Christ. Rayber is steeped in scandal. Evidence from both her narrative and correspondence indicates that is indeed how O'Connor saw it. "Rayber and Tarwater are really fighting the same current in themselves," she comments in a letter. "Rayber wins out against it and Tarwater loses; Rayber achieves his own will and Tarwater submits to his vocation." She even refers to the "Satanic choice" made by Rayber in the novel (*CW*, 1170).

Nonetheless, O'Connor also reveals that the case may not be quite so clear-cut. Perhaps she was not quite finished with Rayber as her stumbling block. She writes in a letter that Rayber's reaction to his Satanic choice "may indicate that he is not going to be able to sustain his choice—but that is another book maybe" (*CW*, 1170). O'Connor did not live to write this other book, but she left some intimations in *The Violent Bear It Away* that help us to understand the complexity of being scandalized and causing scandal.

So Rayber as a stumbling block is a rival to O'Connor herself. She gives, then, an indication in the novel that the story is not so simple as the nephew, Tarwater, losing (winning) and Rayber winning (losing). Tarwater's own story was first played out by Rayber. Many years before Tarwater was kidnapped by his uncle, the prophet, Rayber was also kidnapped, but the old man did nothing to prevent his parents from taking him back. Rayber had four days at the farm named Powderhead; Tarwater had fourteen years. The old man would tell the story of his relationship with Rayber to Tarwater. Usually it was a tale of misunderstanding and betrayal in which Rayber was cast as an educated fool, but sometimes the story would take a different turn.

> There were moments when the thought he might have helped the nephew
> on to his new course [turning away from his true vocation] himself became
> so heavy in the old man that he would stop telling the story to Tarwater,

stop and stare in front of him as if he were looking into a pit which had opened up before his feet.

At such times he would wander into the woods and leave Tarwater alone in the clearing, occasionally for days, while he thrashed out his peace with the Lord, and when he returned, bedraggled and hungry, he would look the way the boy thought a prophet ought to look. He would look as if he had been wrestling a wildcat, as if his head were still full of the vision he had seen in its eyes, wheels of light and strange beasts with giant wings of fire and four heads turned to the points of the universe. (*CW*, 333–34)

The violence of love here means that the prophet has to accept the possibility that he had, in fact, scandalized a little one and that he is dependent on the Lord for mercy in light of that sin. Rayber makes his own choices and bears his own responsibility, but the lines that connect in Christ mean not only that none of us come to Christ on our own but also that none of us walk away from him on our own either. His uncle's failures do not excuse Rayber or take away his present responsibility, but they do implicate the old man in Rayber's loss of faith. O'Connor's struggle with her own stumbling block, Rayber, may not have been at an end.

This is the mystery. A line leads from a tenderness divorced from Christ and surrounded by theory to the gas chambers of totalitarianism. Another line leads from Hawthorne through his daughter and Mary Ann to O'Connor and those who live in Christ. These are two different lines, yet they cross and intersect. We cannot simply divide the world into those who scandalize and those who do not, or into those who are scandalized and those who are not. Instead, we see that in our broken condition even our best efforts can scandalize someone, rendering him or her incapable of seeing beneath the surface. We need, then, forgiveness—the capacity to see the sin or the scandal as a reality that passes now out of existence. Rayber cannot forgive his uncle, and it is a struggle for his uncle to forgive himself. We can fail and be scandalized in either way—not forgiving those who need it, or not letting ourselves be forgiven. Alternatively, we can allow ourselves and the other to be recreated.

Conclusion

We conclude with a story that is meant to serve as a pendant to the story with which we began. We opened with Socrates relating the story of Leontius's encounter with the corpses. Socrates prefaced his telling by saying, "I once heard something that I trust."[1] At the close we have another story relating something that the writer has heard and in which he emphasizes the credibility of what he relates. This story also is an encounter with a corpse, but it brings this scandalous scene to a different end.

[31]Since it was the day of Preparation, the Jews did not want the bodies left on the cross during the sabbath, especially because that sabbath was a day of great solemnity. So they asked Pilate to have the legs of the crucified men broken and the bodies removed. [32]Then the soldiers came and broke the legs of the first and of the other who had been crucified with him. [33]But when they came to Jesus and saw that he was already dead, they did not break his legs. [34]Instead, one of the soldiers pierced his side with a spear, and at once blood and water came out. [35](He who saw this has testified so that you also may believe. His testimony is true, and he knows that he tells the truth.) [36]These things occurred so that the scripture might be fulfilled,

"None of his bones shall be broken." [37] And again another passage of scripture says, "They will look on the one whom they have pierced."

It is hard to understand the act of the soldier as anything other than a literal adding of insult to injury. It was clear that Jesus was dead, so the soldiers did not break his legs. Still, one soldier felt compelled to stab the corpse. Perhaps it was a way of showing that this supposed king, this Messiah was really dead, really rendered powerless. The witness does not allow the intended offense of this act to overwhelm him. Instead he directs his attention to what the mediator, with his spear, literally points at—the corpse. He looks long and hard at the corpse and something flows out from beneath the surface: blood and water. The author records this testimony so that the reader might also believe. What would he have us believe? He would have us believe that these things occurred so that "the scripture might be fulfilled." That is, he would have us believe that in the flowing out of blood and water from the side of Christ the whole meaning of the Old Testament has been fulfilled. We are to believe that all the blood, from the foundation of the world, as it were, has been accounted for in this death. We are to believe that all the waters of all the floods that have been unleashed have been taken into account. All of this violence has been fulfilled or completed on the body of the Son. We are to believe that what flows back from all this violence is one gift with two fruits: the gift of forgiveness with its fruits of communion (the Eucharist) and community (baptism).

The story to which this is a pendant is that of Leontius striving not to look at the corpses and failing. Contrary to Plato's suggestion, Leontius's failure cannot be overcome by a better husbanding of the available forces. And, if we accept Plato's analogy in the *Republic* between the individual soul and the city, neither will the city be better ordered and thus healthier through the application of force. Rather, we have outlined a longer journey that accepts the risk and the reward of looking "long and hard" at the victims of society's violence. The risk is to get caught on the surface. The reward is to understand the real workings of a society through the portal of political violence. The way to the reward is to get "beneath the surface." Certainly there are occasions where it is better not to look directly, but then only so that one can see the reality more deeply. Dante does not look directly at Medusa so that he may look at the depths of hell. And he looks upon them only in order to be able to gaze into the eyes of Beatrice and through and with her into the "love that moves the sun and other stars." The point is not so much to contemplate the scandalous spectacle as to see through it to the transcendent love "which remains invisible beyond the transcendent violence that stands between" (*TH*, 217).

The hermeneutics that I have outlined in these chapters is meant to help the reader get beneath the surface, to move out of the worldview or mindset of the violent lie into an encounter with true transcendence. Leontius's dual desire to look and not to look is characteristic of a scandalized consciousness. The contrast between the kind of desire that either gets caught up in the fascinating spectacle or refuses to see it and the kind of desire that enables one to look and get beneath the surface suggests both a difference and a similarity between the two. Both are desires. At the bottom of the former is some rivalry. The look or the refusal to look is based on an attempt at mastery of the situation or of oneself, with the view of outdoing or surpassing the other. The latter desire is, at root, one of submission—not necessarily to the person of Christ, but to truth or to the demands of one's art, or simply to reality. Such submission, as Flannery O'Connor saw and expressed, makes it possible for even violence to return us to reality, that is, to the non-violent truth of love.

I stress that the difference between the two is not the presence or the lack of rationality. This is not a form of Gnosticism. As the story of Leontius shows, Plato understood that reason alone could not master scandal. His solution was to tap the power of anger to control the desire to look upon the scandalous sight. But the only real solution is a change in consciousness. The release from the misrecognition generated by mimetic rivalry and its inherent violence cannot come from someone who is party to a rivalry over who is free from the misrecognition. Only someone "who is not obliged to violence for anything and does not think in terms of violence" can reveal the truth about violence and the scandal that it generates (*TH*, 218).

Our struggles with scandal never come to an end. A person can work to avoid anything that might cause upset, to stay away from mimetic rivalry and to keep an equilibrium. But insofar as scandal is the moving away from the fascinating object in a way that brings us back to it, all of these maneuvers can end up delivering us more deeply into the *skandalon*. The paradoxical result is that the movements of someone getting more and more entangled in a web may, at times, resemble the movements of someone who is becoming more and more free. Neither movement is linear, but they are heading in opposite directions.

The true movement away from scandal includes a reordering of our interpersonal relations that frees us from rivalry. It is a delivery from the thrall of false or deviated transcendence of violence to an encounter with true transcendence. It is in the nature of our predicament that we are both attracted to and repelled by the truth. Our reason can distinguish between the truth and falsehood but the truth is often hard to accept and this interferes with our recognition of it.

As we have seen throughout, stories or narratives help us in this struggle by teaching us how to interpret or understand in such a way that what seemed to be a stumbling block becomes a bridge. We take up an attitude toward texts that is in some ways analogous to the attitude Christ claims is God's own: I desire mercy not sacrifice. We do not sacrifice the texts that scandalize us. As always, this scandal is neither purely in the text nor purely in us but in that space between. We read such texts with a quality of mercy, with forgiveness. Furthermore, this forgiveness is also not unidirectional. It may well be us who need forgiveness but it can also be the text. We interpret these writings with an awareness of what they would have us reject or what we would reject from them. In this way they point us toward either what we would sacrifice from them or what they themselves have rejected. This reveals the dependence of our interpretation on some expulsion or it allows the text to reveal its dependence on *both* the rejection and what was rejected. Restoring what was rejected will undo both ourselves and those writings at the same time that it brings them and us to our true completion.

Notes

Introduction

1. Mark Danner, *Stripping Bare the Body: Politics Violence War* (New York: Nation Books, 2009).

2. Plato, *The Republic of Plato*, 2nd ed., trans. Alan Bloom, book 4, 439e–440a (New York: Basic Books, 1991), 119, translation modified.

3. "Plato—Leontius' Corpses" in *Harper's Magazine*, an online commentary on Scott Horton's interview with Mark Danner.

4. I do not mean to set up some dichotomy here by which seeing becomes associated with being scandalized and listening with getting beneath the surface. For an example of how listening can entrap one in scandal, see Augustine's description of Alyppius's being drawn into the scandal of the gladiatorial games in *Confessions*, book 6, vii.

5. Perhaps the most accessible introduction to Girard's notion of scandal is in the opening chapters of *I See Satan Fall like Lightning* (Maryknoll, NY: Orbis Books, 2001). One can also profitably consult James Alison, *The Joy of Being Wrong: Original Sin through Easter Eyes* (New York: Crossroad Herder, 1998), 140–46, and Gil Bailie, *Violence Unveiled: Humanity at the Crossroads* (New York: Crossroad, 1995), 209–12.

6. René Girard, *Deceit, Desire and the Novel: Self and Other in Literary Structure*, trans. Yvonne Freccero (Baltimore: Johns Hopkins University Press, 1965). "Romantic lie" is a translation of the first words of the original title: *Mensonge romantique et vérité romanesque*. He explains it on pages 15–17, especially in the footnote on pages 16–17.

7. Jacques Derrida, *Writing and Difference* (Chicago: University of Chicago Press, 1978). The comparison appears in the essay "Structure, Sign, and Play in the Discourse of the Human Sciences" (278–93).

8. Ibid., 292. Kevin Hart gives a good analysis of Derrida's take on this comparison and its influence on later interpreters. See his *The Trespass of the Sign: Deconstruction, Theology and Philosophy* (Cambridge: Cambridge University Press, 1989), 117–27.

Chapter 1. The Language of Scandal and the Scandal of Language

1. Stanley Rosen in his commentary on the *Republic* explains: "Socrates claims that the story shows that anger (*tēn orgēn*: the attribute of spiritedness) can make war against desires as one thing opposed to another single thing." *Plato's* Republic: *A Study* (New Haven: Yale University Press, 2005), 155.

2. See Plato, *The Republic of Plato*, trans. Allan Bloom (New York: Basic Books, 1991), 457n30.

3. The standard work on scandal remains Gustav Stählin's *Skandalon: Untersuchungen zur Geschichte eines biblischen Begriffs*, Beiträge zur Förderung christlicher Theologie; 2. Reihe, 24. Bd. (Gütersloh, Germany: C. Bertelsmann, 1930). He also wrote the article on "Scandal" in *Theological Dictionary of the New Testament*, ed. Gerhard Friedrich (Grand Rapids, MI: Wm. B. Eerdmans, 1971), 347ff.

4. For a journalistic excursion through the subject of scandal, see Laura Kipnis, *How to Become a Scandal: Adventures in Bad Behavior* (New York: H. Holt, 2010). For a view from sociology see Ari Adut, *On Scandal: Moral Disturbances in Society, Politics, and Art* (Cambridge: Cambridge University Press, 2008).

5. Walker Percy, *The Message in the Bottle: How Queer Man Is, How Queer Language Is, and What One Has to Do with the Other* (New York: Picador, 2000), 153.

6. Ibid., 155.

7. Ibid., 153–54.

8. Helen Keller, *The Story of My Life* (London: Hodder and Stoughton, 1909), 23–24. This story is analyzed by Walker Percy in *The Message in the Bottle* and by Ernst Cassirer in *An Essay on Man.*

9. This phenomenon is analyzed by René Girard in his first major work, *Deceit, Desire and the Novel: Self and Other in Literary Structure* (Baltimore: Johns Hopkins University Press, 1965).

10. Ingmar Bergman's *Persona* remains one of the most powerful artistic representations of this experience.

11. Bernard Lonergan is very helpful on the "principle of the empty head" in *Method in Theology* (New York: Herder and Herder, 1972).

12. Walker Percy, *Lost in the Cosmos: The Last Self-Help Book* (New York: Farrar, Straus, and Giroux, 1983), 105.

13. Ibid.

14. Ibid.

15. René Girard, *Things Hidden since the Foundation of the World* (London: Athlone Press, 1987) , 100 (hereafter cited parenthetically as *TH*).

16. This is not an idiosyncratic interpretation. See William Franke, *Poetry and Apocalypse: Theological Disclosure of Poetic Language* (Stanford, CA: Stanford University Press, 2009), 139. Franke is commenting on Gian Balsamo's work on Christian epic poetry that is carried out in light of Nietzsche's discovery of archaic religious rites beneath the forms of Attic tragedy.

Chapter 2. The Fascination of Friedrich Nietzsche

1. This work first appeared as *Die Geburt der Tragödie aus dem Geiste der Musik* in 1872 and was reprinted in 1874. A new edition with a foreword by Nietzsche was published in 1886 as *Die Geburt der Tragödie. Oder: Griechenthum und Pessimismus.* The text I have used is from Friedrich Nietzsche, *Sämtliche Werke. Kritische Studienausgabe in 15 Bänden* (München, Germany: hg.v.G.Colli und M.Montinari, 1980). For the English translation I have used *The Birth of Tragedy*, trans. Shaun Whiteside, ed. Michael Tanner (London: Penguin Books, 1993). The parenthetical numbers in the text refer to this translation.

2. René Girard, "Superman in the Underground: Strategies of Madness—Nietzsche, Wagner, and Dostoevsky," *MLN* 91 (1976): 1177. Note that in *The Birth of Tragedy* the mediator is still present. Wagner makes appearances through references to his works toward the end of the treatise.

3. Letter of January 30, 1872 to Ritschl, quoted in M. S. Silk and J. P. Stern, *Nietzsche on Tragedy* (Cambridge: Cambridge University Press, 1981), 91.

4. See "Versuch einer Selbstkritik." especially Par.2: die Wissenschaft unter der Optik des Künstlers zu sehen, die Kunst aber unter der des Lebens . . ." 14. Silk and Stern provide a marvelously comprehensive study of the background and development of *The Birth of Tragedy* (*Nietzsche on Tragedy*). They recognize what they call the "hybrid" nature of the work, but can only explain it in terms of different drives or aims that Nietzsche never succeeded in integrating (189). It is of interest that several times they refer to the work as a "centaur," that is, a monster, a mythical figure of composite makeup. There is something very apposite of this, and at the same time something very wrong. As we shall see, the work deliberately crosses boundaries in terms of genre. It is, to use a word that has become popular, transgressive. But to label the work monstrous is to make it easier for us to simply expel Nietzsche's work one more time. At critical moments of interpretation Silk and Stern prefer to interpret the text mythologically rather than asking to what reality it may refer. The authors justify this by quoting a letter written by Nietzsche in 1870, in which he states that "Scholarship, art and philosophy are now growing together inside me so much that I'll be giving birth to centaurs one day" (see pages 39 and 188). They tend to stay on the surface level of associations for their interpretations rather than looking for necessary connections (see Silk and Stern, *Nietzsche on Tragedy*, 202, where they give their interpretation of the vulture or *Geier* which appears on page 132 of the text). If the reader does not engage the scandal of text, then all one can do is look at the surface riddles (see pages 206–9 for their view the "riddles").

5. John Sallis, *The Birth of Tragedy* in his *Crossings: Nietzsche and the Space of Tragedy* (Chicago: University of Chicago Press, 1991). I am indebted to his development of the idea of "space" for the interpretation of this work. He is also very sensitive to the way in which Nietzsche moves back and forth between extremes. But he also sees all this as a kind of play, a game that one plays with Nietzsche. He does not pursue what lies behind the self-destruction of the text which he so clearly sees (148). He is aware of what he calls the "sliding" of the text from the theoretical to the artistic, but as the word suggests, this sliding is something that occurs under its own weight, and not for a reason (147–49).

6. Boyle has an observation on this that gets to the heart of the matter: "Nietzsche's formula that 'only as an aesthetic phenomenon is the world and existence eternally justified' could not be more wrong; it needs to be reversed, so as to run: only as a revelation that the world and existence matter eternally—matter so much that God who made them died to restore them—is the phenomenon of literature possible. An event of representation is an event of forgiveness, a participation—imperfect, of course—in the divine act, not of creation (as a romantic aesthetics

once maintained), but of re-creation." From *Sacred and Secular Scriptures: A Catholic Approach to Literature* (Notre Dame: Notre Dame University Press, 2005), 133.

7. René Girard, *Violence and the Sacred* (Baltimore: Johns Hopkins University Press, 1977), 134–35.

8. See page 104. Nietzsche is speaking of the very point where tragedy reaches its "supreme goal." He says that it is through the destruction of the "Apollonian deception." This destruction reveals the deception to be "a veiling of the true Dionysian effect, which lasts for the duration of the tragedy." Thus, we need not only to look at the nature of the "veiling," but also to ask after the "true Dionysian effect."

9. Girard, *Violence and the Sacred*, 135.

10. Ibid.

11. Ibid.

12. Ibid., 292.

13. This famous opposition between the Apollonian and Dionsyian begins by comparing their duality to the duality of the sexes (14) and ends in their "fraternal bond" (113). The reversal and undoing of the posited distinction could not be clearer.

14. The brief comment by Ann Astell is apposite: "Nietzschean theory reinstates and defends the same Apollonian-Dionysian myth whereby the violent sacrifice of the one by the many is justified" (from Ann W. Astell, "Nietzsche, Chaucer, and the Sacrifice of Art," in *The Chaucer Review* 39, no. 3 [2005]: 322–40; the quotation is from page 327).

15. There are a number of ways we can read this last quote. Ostensibly, it is a mistake. Dionysus was not torn apart by the Maenads, but by the Titans, as Nietzsche himself reports on page 52. More deeply, it associates Socrates with Pentheus, who is destroyed by the Maenads. But it can also associate Pentheus himself with Dionysus: meaning that Nietzsche saw that the god was created through a form of murder.

16. Girard, *Violence and the Sacred*, 136.

17. Ibid., 137.

18. Ibid., 129.

19. Ibid., 130.

20. Ibid.

21. Ibid., 138.

Chapter 3. The Scandal of Jean-Jacques Rousseau

1. Eric Gans, "The Victim as Subject: The Esthetico-Ethical System of Rousseau's *Rêveries*," in *Jean-Jacques Rousseau*, ed. Harold Bloom (New York: Chelsea House Publishers, 1988), 215.

2. In the *Confessions* Rousseau writes that Diderot urged him to compete for the prize. "I did so, and from that instant I was lost. All the rest of my life and misfortunes was the inevitable effect of that instant of aberration" (*CW* 5:295). A note on the references to Rousseau's texts: For the French text of Rousseau's works I have used *Oeuvres completes*, vols. 1–5 (Paris: NRF-Edition de la Pléiade, 1959–95). All translations are taken from *Collected Writings of Rousseau*, 13 vols., ed. Roger D. Masters and Christopher Kelly (Hanover, NH.: University Press of New England, 1991–2010). I cite this source as *CW* with the volume and page number following.

3. I use "Controversy" with a capital letter here as a technical term to refer to those writings by Rousseau and his opponents that followed publication of the *First Discourse.*

4. Claude Levi-Strauss, "Rousseau, Father of Anthropology," *The Unesco Courier* 16.3 (1963): 10.

5. While it is true that Rousseau never used the term "noble savage," it does capture an important aspect of his thought.

6. For a more detailed analysis of the text, see my *A Reinterpretation of Rousseau: A Religious System* (New York: Palgrave, 2007), 114–17.

7. Again, see my extended analysis of this phrase in Alberg, *A Reinterpretation of Rousseau,* 120–23.

8. For an in-depth discussion of the doctrine of Original Sin from which I have learned much, see James Alison, *The Joy of Being Wrong: Original Sin through Easter Eyes* (New York: Crossroad, 1998).

9. The most thoroughly developed of these attempts is Arthur Melzer's *The Natural Goodness of Man: On the System of Rousseau's Thought* (Chicago: University of Chicago Press, 1990).

10. See Robert J. Ellrich, *Rousseau and His Reader: The Rhetorical Situation of the Major Works* (Chapel Hill: University of North Carolina Press, 1969). Ellrich sees this sentence as evidence of Rousseau's "fundamental posture in the work, his presentation of himself to the reader as the virtuous outsider" (28).

11. Frédéric S. Eigeldinger, "Ils ne me pardonneront jamais le mal qu'ils m'ont fait," in *Etudes Jean-Jacques Rousseau* 10 (1998): 77–89.

12. *CW* 12:67; Pl. 1:1183–4. See Eigeldinger, "Ils ne me pardonneront jamais le mal qu'ils m'ont fait," 78.

13. Rousseau wrote this letter as a public response to Archbishop Christophe de Beaumont's *Mandement* or Pastoral Letter condemning *Emile.* An English translation of the *Mandement* is available in *CW* 9:3–16.

14. Quoted in Eigeldinger, "Ils ne me pardonneront jamais le mal qu'ils m'ont fait," (page 86) from 6 avril 1765, *CC* 4252. Original text: "Après avoir établi en principe leur compétence sur tout scandale, . . . excitent le scandale sur tel objet qui leur plait, et puis en vertu de ce scandale qui est leur ouvrage. . . . s'emparent de l'affaire pour la juger": "[. . . Les brouillons de ministres [de Neuchâtel] me haïssent encore plus à cause du mal qu'ils n'ont pu me faire."

15. Nicholas Boyle, *Sacred and Secular Scriptures: A Catholic Approach to Literature* (Notre Dame: University of Notre Dame Press, 2005), 144.

16. Ibid.

17. Ibid.

18. Ibid.

19. It seems to me that this is what Reinhard Hütter means when he interprets St. Thomas as holding that, in order to understand, the will must first be healed of its incurvature. That we need a healing of the will is suggested to us by the contrast in the parable of the ungrateful servant. He, being forgiven a massive debt by his Lord, then turned around and demanded the few dollars owed to him by his fellow servant. Our own experience of forgiveness is to produce a will that is ready to forgive that which is owed to us. See Hütter's article "The Directedness of Reasoning and the Metaphysics of Creation," in Paul J. Griffiths and Reinhard Hütter, eds., *Reason and the Reasons of*

Faith (New York: T and T Clark, 2005). The whole collection is worth consulting, as many of its outstanding articles touch on topics related to this book.

20. M. Gautier was a professor of mathematics and history who published his "Refutation of the Discourse Which Won the Prize of the Academy of Dijon in 1750" in the *Mercury of France* in October of 1751. Rousseau published his reply as letter addressed to his erstwhile friend, Friedrich Melchior, baron von Grimm in a brochure in November of 1751.

21. Formerly known as Stanislaus I (1677–1766), he was the deposed King of Poland. His piece was published anonymously. Rousseau assumed that it was written at least in part by his Jesuit advisor Father de Menou (see *Confessions CW* 5:307).

22. The image can be found at http://rivendell.forumactif.com/t492-la-torture-au-moyen-age.

23. This analysis is subtly confirmed by an incident in Dante's *Inferno*. In Canto XXIII Dante and Virgil are walking through the malebolge in which the hypocrites are punished. These hypocrites walk along slowly, wearing heavy stoles which are lead, gilded with gold. The meaning of the punishment is clear: these men appeared virtuous and upright, while in fact being duplicitous and evil, so now they appear richly adorned but in fact are simply weighed down and made tired by their outfits. Hypocrisy makes one cautious—the truth is not to be revealed and so their interior lack of spontaneity is given an objective correlative. In this circle of Hell, Dante meets one man who had belonged to the order of *Frati Godeni*, a Christian community that was notorious for its laxness and he begins to enunciate his judgment of these sinners: "I began, O brothers, your ill-doing . . . / But I said no more for there ran to my eyes the sight of one crucified with stakes upon the ground." The "one crucified" is Caiaphas, the high priest who condemned Jesus to death with the familiar principle (a principle vigorously opposed by Rousseau, I might add): "It is better to have one man die for the people than to have the whole nation destroyed" (Jn. 11:50). Dante had been about to begin a denunciation of the hypocrites he had just encountered, but his words break off. In the sight of the Cross one cannot remain in the world of condemning and being condemned, that is the Old Law, from which the Cross is to redeem us. And Virgil says nothing at all. Robin Kirkpatrick comments: Virgil as the representative of reason, "can understand neither grace nor the history in which the high priest Caiaphas was an actor—of the Passion of Christ; he cannot see what is at stake" (*Dante's Inferno: Difficulty and Dead Poetry* [Cambridge: Cambridge University Press, 1988], 283).

24. John Freccero, *Dante: The Poetics of Conversion* (Cambridge: Harvard University Press, 1986), 122.

25. William Franke, *Dante's Interpretive Journey* (Chicago: University of Chicago Press, 1996), 3.

26. *CW* 1. For an extended analysis of this difficult work, see Alberg, *A Reinterpretation of Rousseau*, 19–37.

27. For an interpretation of his writings from the viewpoint of accusing and being accused, see Jean Starobinski, "The Accuser and the Accused," in *Jean-Jacques Rousseau*, ed. Harold Bloom (New York: Chelsea House Publishers, 1988), 173–93.

Chapter 4. The Interpretation of Dante Alighieri

1. For a discussion of direct address and its use by Dante, see William Franke, *Dante's Interpretive Journey* (Chicago: University of Chicago Press, 1996), 37–81. For a discussion of the passage from *The Divine Comedy* that I quote, see John Freccero, "Medusa: The Letter and the Spirit," in *Dante: The Poetics of Conversion*, ed. Rachel Jacoff (Cambridge: Harvard University Press, 1986), 119–35.

2. For Dante's text I have used the *Inferno*, ed. and trans. Charles Singleton (Princeton: Princeton University Press, 1980).

3. Franke, *Dante's Interpretive Journey*, 90.

4. Freccero, *Dante: The Poetics of Conversion*, 121.

5. Ibid., *121*, 121.

6. Ibid., 121, 119.

7. Ibid., 121, 120.

8. Hence, he intends both the *Discourse on Inequality* and *Emile* as a "history of [our] species" (*CW* 3:19, 13:599).

9. For a fuller discussion of this move by Rousseau, see Alberg, *A Reinterpretation of Rousseau*, 120–23.

10. Freccero, *Dante: The Poetics of Conversion*, 122.

11. Ibid., 121, 133.

12. Freccero comments on this: "[F]or it was her feminine *beauty* that constituted the mortal threat to her admirers. From the ancient *Physiologus* through the mythographers to Boccaccio, the Medusa represented a sensual fascination, a *pulchritude* so excessive that it turned men to stone" (125).

13. *The Poetics of Conversion*, 121, 129.

14. Ibid., 121, 130.

15. Franke, *Dante's Interpretive Journey*, 85n2.

16. See John Freccero, "The Fig Tree and the Laurel: Petrarch's Poetics," *Diacritics* 5. 1 (1975): 34–40.

17. Freccero, *Dante: The Poetics of Conversion*, 121.

18. Ibid., 121.

19. This translation is by James Marchand of the University of Illinois. It was accessed at http://www9.georgetown.edu/faculty/jod/cangrande.english.html.

20. For the history and development of this kind of interpretation, see Henri de Lubac, *Medieval Exegesis*, vols. 1 and 2 (Edinburgh: T and T Clark, 1998).

21. The following is my adaptation of this insight from James Alison, *The Joy of Being Wrong: Original Sin through Easter Eyes* (New York: Crossroads, 1998), especially 7–9.

22. See Paul Griffiths and Reinhard Hütter, *Reason and the Reasons of Faith* (London: T and T Clark, 2005), for an outstanding collection of essays on the way in which faith transforms reason.

23. For this understanding of "scandal," see Søren Kierkegaard, *The Sickness unto Death*, trans. Howard V. Hong and Edna H. Hong (Princeton: Princeton University Press, 1980). For an excellent work on scandal in the New Testament, see David McCracken's *The Scandal of the Gospels: Jesus, Story, and Offense* (Oxford: Oxford University Press, 1994).

Chapter 5. The Lesson of the Gospels

1. In speaking about Rousseau's *Social Contract*, Girard makes the following comment: "The continuing fascination of the *Social Contract* is owing not to the truths it may contain but to

the dizzying oscillation it maintains between these two forces." The "two forces" refer to the crowd and to the established rulers—in other words, to the periphery and to the center. Girard continues, "Instead of resolutely choosing one and holding to that choice, like the rational members of all parties, Rousseau wanted to reconcile the irreconcilable; his work is somewhat like the disturbance of a real revolution, incompatible with the great principles it expresses" (*The Scapegoat* [Baltimore: Johns Hopkins University Press, 1986], 115).

2. The notion of occupying the "place of shame" is borrowed from James Alison. It is a central concept in many of his writings. See *Undergoing God: Dispatches from the Scene of a Break-In* (New York: Continuum, 2006).

3. In his excellent book *Saved From Sacrifice: A Theology of the Cross* (Grand Rapids: Wm. B. Eerdmans, 2006) S. Mark Heim often returns to this theme. Early on, he puts it this way: "to explain how something of surpassing value with only a subtle twist becomes a twin of almost opposite character and effects, or how a teaching that rightly merits rejection might still contain rare and profound truths we lose at our peril—these things are hard to do" (ix).

4. For some profound reflections on this theme, see James Alison's "The Man Blind from Birth and the Creator's Subversion of Sin," in *Faith beyond Resentment: Fragments Catholic and Gay* (New York: Crossroad, 2001), 3–26.

5. I am trying to stay as close to the Greek as I can in this case. It is translated as "Blessed is the man who does fall away on account of me" in the NIV and "Blessed is he who takes no offense at me" in the RSV.

6. Frank Kermode, *The Genesis of Secrecy: On the Interpretation of Narrative* (Cambridge: Harvard University Press, 1979), 29.

7. Ibid., 30.

8. Ibid..

9. Ibid., 47.

10. See his *Letter to d'Alembert on the Theater* (*CW*, 10), especially page 259.

11. See again, Alison, *Faith beyond Resentment*.

12. For a slightly different treatment of the story of the Good Samaritan, one from which I learned much, see Andrew J. McKenna, *Violence and Difference: Girard, Derrida, and Deconstruction* (Urbana: University of Illinois Press, 1992), 211–21.

13. See Turid Karlsen Seim, *The Double Message: Patterns of Gender in Luke-Acts* (Nashville: Abingdon, 1994).

Chapter 6. The Challenge of Flannery O'Connor

1. Flannery O'Connor, *Collected Works of Flannery O'Connor*, edited by Sally Fitzgerald (New York: Library of America, 1988), 805–6. Hereafter *CW*.

2. See the letter addressed to Eileen Hall, editor of the book page for *The Bulletin*, a diocesan paper for which O'Connor wrote many book reviews. O'Connor had been asked about the problem of "scandalizing the 'little ones.'" She replied that she had asked a priest about this once, and his immediate response was that "You don't have to write for fifteen-year-old girls." O'Connor's problem, however, was that "the mind of a fifteen-year-old girl lurks in many a head that is

seventy-five and people are every day being scandalized not only by what is scandalous of its nature but by what is not" (*CW*, 987).

3. Flannery O'Connor, *Mystery and Manners: Occasional Prose*, ed. Sally Fitzgerald and Robert Fitzgerald (New York: Farrar, Straus and Giroux, 1969), 80. In a letter she also writes, "I suppose when I say that the moral basis of Poetry is the accurate naming of the things of God, I mean about the same thing that Conrad meant when he said that his aim as an artist was to render the highest possible justice to the visible universe" (*CW*, 981).

4. *CW*, 81.

5. For a complementary view of O'Connor's art as representing the dynamic relationship between Word and Art, see Albert Sonnenfeld's "Flannery O'Connor: The Catholic Writer as Baptist," *Contemporary Literature* 13.4 (Autumn 1972).

6. *CW*, 82.

7. Ibid., 83.

8. Ibid., 113.

9. Ibid., 112.

10. Girard writes in a similar vein: "Romantic liberalism is the father of destructive nihilism" (*Deceit, Desire and the Novel: Self and Other in Literary Structure*, trans. Yvonne Freccero [Baltimore: Johns Hopkins University Press, 1965], 254).

11. René Girard, *"To Double Business Bound": Essays on Literature, Mimesis, and Anthropology* (Baltimore: Johns Hopkins University Press, 1988), 2.

12. Girard, *Deceit, Desire and the Novel*, 158.

Conclusion

1. Plato, *The Republic of Plato*, trans. Alan Bloom, Book IV, 439e (New York: Basic Books, 1991), 119.

Bibliography

Adut, Ari. *On Scandal: Moral Disturbances in Society, Politics, and Art*. New York: Cambridge University Press, 2008.

Alberg, Jeremiah. *A Reinterpretation of Rousseau: A Religious System*. New York: Palgrave, 2007.

Alison, James. *Undergoing God: Dispatches from the Scene of a Break-In*. New York: Continuum, 2006.

———. *Faith Beyond Resentment: Fragments Catholic and Gay*. New York: Crossroad, 2001.

———. *The Joy of Being Wrong: Original Sin through Easter Eyes*. New York: Crossroad, 1998.

Ambrosiano, Jason. "'From the Blood of Abel to His Own': Intersubjectivity and Salvation in Flannery O'Connor's *The Violent Bear It Away*." *Flannery O'Connor Review* (2007): 130–40.

Ansell-Pearson, Keith. *Nietzsche Contra Rousseau: A Study of Nietzsche's Moral and Political Thought*. New York: Cambridge University Press, 1991.

Archer, Emily. "'Stalking Joy': Flannery O'Connor's Accurate Naming." *Religion Literature* 18.2 (1986): 17–30.

Asals, Frederick. "Differentiation, Violence, and the Displaced Person." *The Flannery O'Connor Bulletin* 13 (1984): 1–14.

Astell, Ann W. "Nietzsche, Chaucer, and the Sacrifice of Art." *The Chaucer Review* 39.3 (2005): 323–40.

Augustine. *Confessions*, trans. Henry Chadwick. New York: Oxford University Press, 1992.

Bailie, Gil. *Violence Unveiled: Humanity at the Crossroads*. New York: Crossroad, 1995.

Bergup, O. S. B., Bernice. "Themes of Redemptive Grace in the Works of Flannery O'Connor: A Theological Inquiry." *The American Benedictine Review* 21.2 (1970): 175–80.

Bolton, Betsy. "Placing Violence, Embodying Grace: Flannery O'Connor's 'Displaced Person.'" *Studies in Short Fiction* 34.1 (Winter 1997).

Borody, Wayne A. "Nietzsche on the Cross: The Defence of Personal Freedom in the Birth of Tragedy." *Humanitas* 16.2 (2003): 76–93.

Boyle, Nicholas. *Sacred and Secular Scriptures: A Catholic Approach to Literature.* Notre Dame: University of Notre Dame Press, 2005.

Brinkmeyer, Robert H., Jr. "Borne Away by Violence: The Reader and Flannery O'Connor." *Southern Review* 15.2 (1965): 313–21.

Cassirer, Ernst. *An Essay on Man: An Introduction to a Philosophy of Human Culture.* New Haven: Yale University Press, 1944.

Ciuba, Gary M. *Desire, Violence, and Divinity in Modern Southern Fiction: Katherine Anne Porter, Flannery O'Connor, Cormac McCarthy, Walker Percy.* Baton Rouge: Louisiana State University Press, 2007.

———. "'Like a Boulder Blocking Your Path': Scandal and Skandalon in Flannery O'Connor." *The Flannery O'Connor Bulletin* 26–27 (2000): 1–23.

Clegg, Jerry S. "Mann Contra Nietzsche." *Philosophy and Literature* 28.1 (April 2004): 157–64.

Cofer, Jordan R. Review of *Desire, Violence, and Divinity in Modern Southern Fiction: Katherine Ann Porter, Flannery O'Connor, Cormac McCarthy, Walker Percy. Southern Quarterly* 46.1 (Fall 2008): 177–80.

Danner, Mark. *Stripping Bare the Body: Politics Violence War.* New York: Nation Books, 2009.

Dante. *Inferno,* trans. and ed. Charles Singleton. Princeton: Princeton University Press, 1980.

de Lubac, Henri. *Medieval Exegesis,* vols. 1 and 2. Edinburgh: T&T Clark, 1998.

Derrida, Jacques. *Of Grammatology.* Baltimore: Johns Hopkins University Press, 1998.

———. *Writing and Difference.* Chicago: University of Chicago Press, 1978.

Desmond, John F. "Violence and the Christian Mystery: A Way To Read Flannery O'Connor." *Literature and Belief* 15 (1995): 163–81.

———. "The Mystery of the Word and the Act: *The Violent Bear It Away.*" *The American Benedictine Review* 24.3 (1973): 342–47.

Devir, Nathan P. "Apollo/Dionysus or Heraclitus/Anaxagoras? A Hermeneutic Inquiry into Nietzsche's View of Tragedy." *Papers on Language and Literature* 46.1 (Winter 2010): 61–78.

Duncan, John. "Culture, Tragedy and Pessimism in Nietzsche's Birth of Tragedy." *PhaenEx: Journal of Existential and Phenomenological Theory and Culture* 1.2 (October 2006): 47–70.

Eigeldinger, Frédéric S. "Ils ne me pardonneront jamais le mal qu'ils m'ont fait." *Etudes Jean-Jacques Rousseau* 10 (1998).

Eigen, Michael. "The Sword of Grace: Flannery O'Connor, Wilfred R. Bion and D. W. Winnicott." *The Psychoanalytic Review* 72 (1985): 335–46.

Ellrich, Robert J. *Rousseau and His Reader: The Rhetorical Situation of the Major Works.* Chapel Hill: University of North Carolina Press, 1969.

Fields, Stephen. "The Beauty of the Ugly: Balthasar, the Crucifixion, Analogy and God." *International Journal of Systematic Theology* 9.2 (2007): 172–83.

Franke, William. *Poetry and Apocalypse: Theological Disclosure of Poetic Language.* Stanford, CA: Stanford University Press, 2009.

———. *Dante's Interpretive Journey.* Chicago: Chicago University Press, 1996.

Freccero, John. *Dante: The Poetics of Conversion,* ed. Rachel Jacoff. Cambridge: Harvard University Press, 1986.

———. "The Fig Tree and the Laurel: Petrarch's Poetics." *Diacritics* 5.1 (Spring 1975): 34–40.

Frederick, Asals. "Differentiation, Violence, and the Displaced Person." *The Flannery O'Connor Bulletin* 13 (1984): 1–14.

Gans, Erich. "The Victim as Subject: The Esthetico-Ethical System of Rousseau's *Rêveries.*" In *Jean-Jacques Rousseau,* ed. Harold Bloom. New York: Chelsea House Publishers, 1988.

Girard, René. *Deceit, Desire and the Novel: Self and Other in Literary Structure,* trans. Yvonne Freccero. Baltimore: Johns Hopkins University Press, 1965.

———. "Dionysus Versus the Crucified." *MLN* 99.4 (September 1984): 816–35.

———. "João Cezar de Castro Rocha, and Pierpaolo Antonello." *Evolution and Conversion: Dialogues on the Origins of Culture.* New York: T & T Clark, 2007.

———. *Job, the Victim of His People.* London: Athlone Press, 1987.

———. *The Scapegoat.* Baltimore: Johns Hopkins University Press, 1986.

———. "Superman in the Underground: Strategies of Madness—Nietzsche, Wagner, and Dostoevsky." *MLN* 91.6 (December 1976): 1161–85.

———. *"To Double Business Bound": Essays on Literature, Mimesis, and Anthropology.* Baltimore: Johns Hopkins University Press, 1988.

———. *Violence and the Sacred.* Baltimore: Johns Hopkins University Press, 1979.

Girard, René, and Benoît Chantre. *Battling to the End: Conversations with Benoît Chantre.* East Lansing: Michigan State University Press, 2010.

Girard, René, and Robert Doran. *Mimesis and Theory: Essays on Literature and Criticism, 1953–2005.* Stanford: Stanford University Press, 2008.

Girard, René, Jean-Michel Oughourlian, and Guy Lefort. *Things Hidden since the Foundation of the World.* London: Athlone Press, 1987.

Girard, René, and James G. Williams. *The Girard Reader.* New York: Crossroad, 2002.

———. *I See Satan Fall like Lightning.* Maryknoll, NY: Orbis Books, 2001.

Griffiths, Paul J. *Religious Reading: The Place of Reading in the Practice of Religion.* New York: Oxford University Press, 1999.

Griffiths, Paul J., and Reinhard Hütter. *Reason and the Reasons of Faith.* New York: T and T Clark, 2005.

Han-Pile, Beatrice. "Nietzsche's Metaphysics in *the Birth of Tragedy.*" *European Journal of Philosophy* 14.3 (December 2006): 373–403.

Harper's Magazine. *"Plato—Leontius's Corpses,"* an on-line commentary on interview with Mark Danner. Available from http://www.harpers.org/archive/2009/10/hbc-90006008/.

Hart, Kevin. *The Trespass of the Sign: Deconstruction, Theology and Philosophy.* Cambridge: Cambridge University Press, 1989.

Heim, S. Mark. *Saved from Sacrifice: A Theology of the Cross.* Grand Rapids, MI: Wm. B. Eerdmans, 2006.

Henrichs, Albert. "Loss of Self, Suffering, Violence: The Modern View of Dionysus from Nietzsche to Girard." *Harvard Studies in Classical Philology* 88 (1984): 205–40.

Jacobs, Alan. *A Theology of Reading: The Hermeneutics of Love.* Boulder: Westview Press, 2001.

Kane, Richard. "Positive Destruction in the Fiction of Flannery O'Connor." *The Southern Literary Journal* 1.1 (Autumn 1968): 45–60.

Katz, Claire. "Flannery O'Connor's Rage of Vision." *American Literature* 46.1 (March 1974): 54–67.

Keller, Hellen. *The Story of My Life.* New York: Doubleday, 1954.

Kermode, Frank. *The Genesis of Secrecy: On the Interpretation of Narrative.* Cambridge: Harvard University Press, 1979.

Kierkegaard, Søren. *The Sickness unto Death*, trans. Howard V. Hong and Edna H. Hong. Princeton: Princeton University Press, 1980.

Kipnis, Laura. *How to become a Scandal: Adventures in Bad Behavior.* New York: H. Holt, 2010.

Kirkpatrick, Robin. *Dante's Inferno: Difficulty and Dead Poetry.* Cambridge: Cambridge University Press, 1988.

Kittel, Gerhard, Geoffrey William Bromiley, and Gerhard Friedrich. *Theological Dictionary of the New Testament.* Grand Rapids, MI: Wm. B. Eerdmans, 1971.

Levi-Strauss, Claude. "Rousseau, Father of Anthropology." *The Unesco Courier* 16.3 (1963).

Lonergan, Bernard. *Method in Theology.* New York: Herder and Herder, 1972.

———. *Insight: A Study of Human Understanding*, 2nd ed. London: Darton, Longman and Todd, 1957.

Marchand, James. *Dante to Cangrande: English Version.* Available from http://www9.georgetown.edu/faculty/jod/cangrande.english.html.

McCracken, David. *The Scandal of the Gospels: Jesus, Story, and Offense.* Oxford: Oxford University Press, 1994.

McEntyre, Marilyn Chandler. "Mercy that Burns: Violence and Revelation in Flannery O'Connor's Fiction." *Theology Today* 53.3 (October 1996): 331–44.

McHugh, Patrick. "The Birth of Tragedy from the Spirit of the Blues: Philosophy and History in If I Forget Thee, Jerusalem." *The Faulkner Journal* 14.2 (Spring 1999): 57–73.

McKenna, Andrew J. *Violence and Difference: Girard, Derrida, and Deconstruction.* Urbana: University of Illinois Press, 1992.

Meier, John P. "John the Baptist in Matthew's Gospel." *Journal of Biblical Literature* 99.3 (1980): 383–405.

Melzer, Arthur. *The Natural Goodness of Man: On the System of Rousseau's Thought.* Chicago: Chicago University Press, 1990.

Mostefai, Ourida, and John T. Scott. *Rousseau and L'infâme: Religion, Toleration, and Fanaticism in the Age of Enlightenment.* Amsterdam: Rodopi, 2009.

Nietzsche, Friedrich. *The Birth of Tragedy Out of the Spirit of Music*, trans. Shaun Whiteside, ed. Michael Tanner. London: Penguin Books, 1993.

Ochs, Peter. *Peirce, Pragmatism and the Logic of Scripture.* Cambridge: Cambridge University Press, 1998.

O'Connor, Flannery. *Collected Works of Flannery O'Connor,* ed. Sally Fitzgerald. New York: Library of America, 1988.

———. *Mystery and Manners: Occasional Prose,* ed. Sally Fitzgerald and Robert Fitzgerald. New York: Farrar, Straus and Giroux, 1969.

Olson, Steven. "Tarwater's Hats." *Studies in the Literary Imagination* 20.2 (Fall 1987): 37–49.

Percy, Walker. *Lost in the Cosmos: The Last Self-Help Book.* New York: Farrar, Straus, and Giroux, 1983.

———. *The Message in the Bottle: How Queer Man Is, How Queer Language Is, and What One Has to Do with the Other.* New York: Picador, 2000.

Peters, Jason. "The Source of Flannery O'Connor's 'Flung' Fish in *The Violent Bear It Away.*" *ANQ* 18.4 (Fall 2005): 48–53.

Plato. *The Republic of Plato,* 2nd ed., trans. Allan Bloom. New York: Basic Books, 1991.

Ramsey, David. "Political Prophecy? Some Notes on Flannery O'Connor's *The Violent Bear It Away.*" *The Flannery O'Connor Bulletin* 26–27 (1998–2000): 193–201.

Rosen, Stanley. *Plato's Republic: A Study.* New Haven: Yale University Press, 2005.

Rousseau, Jean-Jacques. *Collected Writings of Rousseau,* ed. Roger D. Masters and Christopher Kelly, vol. 13. Hanover, NH: University Press of New England, 1991–.

———. *Œuvres Complètes.* Paris: Gallimard, 1959.

Rousseau, Jean-Jacques, Alembert, Jean Le Rond d', and Allan David Bloom. *Politics and the Arts: Letter to M. D'alembert on the Theatre.* Ithaca: Cornell University Press, 1960.

Sallis, John. *Crossings: Nietzsche and the Space of Tragedy.* Chicago: University of Chicago Press, 1991.

Saunders, Max. *Self Impression: Life-Writing, Autobiografiction, and the Forms of Modern Literature.* Oxford: Oxford University Press, 2010.

Scullin, Kathleen. "Transforming Violence in O'Connor's *The Violent Bear It Away.*" In *Wagering on Transcendence: The Search for Meaning in Literature,* ed. Phyllis Carey. Kansas City, MO: Sheed and Ward, 1997.

Seim, Turid Karlsen. *The Double Message: Patterns of Gender in Luke-Acts.* Nashville: Abington, 1994.

Sherry, Patrick J. "Saying and Showing: Art, Literature and Religious Understanding." *Modern Theology* 18.1 (January 2002): 37–48.

Shinn, Thelma J. "Flannery O'Connor and the Violence of Grace." *Contemporary Literature* 9.1 (1968): 58–73.

Silk, M. S., and J. P. Stern. *Nietzsche on Tragedy.* Cambridge: Cambridge University Press, 1981.

Smith, Francis J. *O'Connor's Religious Viewpoint in* The Violent Bear It Away *Renascence* 22 (1970): 108–12.

Sonnenfeld, Albert. "Flannery O'Connor: The Catholic Writer as Baptist." *Contemporary Literature* 13.4 (Autumn 1972): 445–57.

Spaemann, Robert. *Happiness and Benevolence.* Notre Dame: University of Notre Dame Press, 2000.

———. *Rousseau: Bürger Ohne Vaterland.* Munich: Piper, 1980.

Stählin, Gustav. *Skandalon: Untersuchungen Zu Geschichte Eines Biblischen Begriffs.* Beiträge zur Förderung christlicher Theologie; 2. Reihe, 24. Bd. Gütersloh, Germany: C. Bertelsmann, 1930.

Starobinski, Jean. "The Accuser and the Accused." In *Jean-Jacques Rousseau*, ed. Allan David Bloom. New York: Chelsea House Publishers, 1988.

———. *Jean-Jacques Rousseau: Transparency and Obstruction*, trans. Arthur Goldhammer. Chicago: University of Chicago Press, 1988.

Vattimo, Gianni, René Girard, and Pierpaolo Antonello. *Christianity, Truth, and Weakening Faith: A Dialogue.* New York: Columbia University Press, 2010.

Webb, Chris. "The Violent Are Gored: O'Connor's Theory of Violence in 'Greenleaf.'" *Plaza: Dialogues in Language and Literature* 1.1 (Spring 2011): 36–41.

Wilson, Carol Y. "Family as Affliction, Family as Promise in *The Violent Bear It Away*." *Studies in the Literary Imagination* 20.2 (Fall 1987): 77–86.

Wynne, Judith F. "The Sacramental Irony of Flannery O'Connor." *The Southern Literary Journal* 7.2 (Spring 1975): 33–49.

Young, Julian. "Richard Wagner and the Birth of *The Birth of Tragedy*." *RIPH* 16.2 (January 2008): 217–45.

Subject Index

Index of Scripture Passages